History of Knights Templar

Compiled by
Eldon Mcmillian

Scribbles

Year of Publication 2018

ISBN : 9789352979370

Book Published by

Scribbles

(An Imprint of Alpha Editions)

email - alphaedis@gmail.com

Produced by: PediaPress GmbH
Limburg an der Lahn
Germany
http://pediapress.com/

The content within this book was generated collaboratively by volunteers. Please be advised that nothing found here has necessarily been reviewed by people with the expertise required to provide you with complete, accurate or reliable information. Some information in this book may be misleading or simply wrong. Alpha Editions and PediaPress does not guarantee the validity of the information found here. If you need specific advice (for example, medical, legal, financial, or risk management) please seek a professional who is licensed or knowledgeable in that area.

Sources, licenses and contributors of the articles and images are listed in the section entitled "References". Parts of the books may be licensed under the GNU Free Documentation License. A copy of this license is included in the section entitled "GNU Free Documentation License"

The views and characters expressed in the book are those of the contributors and his/her imagination and do not represent the views of the Publisher.

Contents

Articles   **1**

Introduction   **1**
    Knights Templar 1

History   **23**
    History of the Knights Templar 23
    Chinon Parchment 39

Organization   **45**
    List of Knights Templar 45
    Grand Masters of the Knights Templar 61

Legacy   **67**
    List of Knights Templar sites 67
    International Organisation of Good Templars 73
    Knights Templar (Freemasonry) 79

Appendix   **91**
    References 91
    Article Sources and Contributors 97
    Image Sources, Licenses and Contributors 98

Article Licenses   **101**

Index   **103**

Introduction

Knights Templar

- **Knights Templar**
- **Poor Fellow-Soldiers of Christ and of the Temple of Solomon**
- *Pauperes commilitones Christi Templique Salomonici Hierosolymitanis*

A Seal of the Knights Templar

Active	c. 1119 – c. 1312
Allegiance	The Pope
Type	Catholic military order
Role	Protection of Christian Pilgrims
Size	15,000–20,000 members at peak, 10% of whom were knights[1]
Headquarters	Temple Mount, Jerusalem, Kingdom of Jerusalem
Nickname(s)	<ul><li>*Order of Solomon's Temple*</li><li>*Order Of Christ*</li></ul>
Patron	Saint Bernard of Clairvaux
Motto(s)	<ul><li>*Non nobis, Domine, non nobis, sed Nomini tuo da gloriam*</li><li>(English: Not unto us, O Lord, not unto us, but unto thy Name give glory)</li></ul>
Attire	White mantle with a red cross
Mascot(s)	Two knights riding a single horse

Engagements	The Crusades, including: • Siege of Ascalon (1153) • Battle of Montgisard (1177) • Battle of Marj Ayyun (1179) • Battle of Hattin (1187) • Siege of Acre (1190–1191) • Battle of Arsuf (1191) • Siege of Al-Dāmūs (1210) • Battle of Legnica (1241) • Siege of Acre (1291) • Reconquista
Commanders	
First Grand Master	Hugues de Payens
Last Grand Master	Jacques de Molay

Part of a series on the
Knights Templar

Poor Fellow-Soldiers of Christ and of the Temple of Solomon
Overview
• History • Latin Rule • Seal • Grand Masters • Members • Trials and dissolution
Papal bulls
• *Omne datum optimum* (1139) • *Milites Templi* (1144) • *Militia Dei* (1145) • *Pastoralis praeeminentiae* (1307) • *Faciens misericordiam* (1308) • *Ad providam* (1312) • *Vox in excelso* (1312)
Locations
• France • England • Scotland • Spain • Portugal

Successors
• ▪▪ Sovereign Military Order of Malta • ▪ Order of Christ • ▪ Supreme Order of Christ • ▪ Order of Montesa
Cultural references
• Non nobis • Baphomet • In popular culture
See also
• Military order (monastic society) • Category:Catholic chivalric orders
▪ Catholicism portal
• v • t • e[2]

The **Poor Fellow-Soldiers of Christ and of the Temple of Solomon** (Latin: *Pauperes commilitones Christi Templique Salomonici*), also known as the **Order of Solomon's Temple**, the **Knights Templar** or simply as **Templars**, were a Catholic military order recognised in 1139 by papal bull *Omne Datum Optimum* of the Holy See.[3] The order was founded in 1119 and was active until about 1312.

The order, which was among the wealthiest and most powerful, became a favoured charity throughout Christendom and grew rapidly in membership and power. They were prominent in Christian finance. Templar knights, in their distinctive white mantles with a red cross, were among the most skilled fighting units of the Crusades. Non-combatant members of the order, who formed as much as 90% of the order's members,[1] managed a large economic infrastructure throughout Christendom, developing innovative financial techniques that were an early form of banking,[4,5] building its own network of nearly 1,000 commanderies and fortifications across Europe and the Holy Land, and arguably forming the world's first multinational corporation.

The Templars were closely tied to the Crusades; when the Holy Land was lost, support for the order faded. Rumours about the Templars' secret initiation ceremony created distrust, and King Philip IV of France – deeply in debt to the order – took advantage of the situation to gain control over them. In 1307, he had many of the order's members in France arrested, tortured into giving false confessions, and burned at the stake.[6] Pope Clement V disbanded the order in 1312 under pressure from King Philip.

The abrupt reduction in power of a significant group in European society gave rise to speculation, legend, and legacy through the ages.

Figure 1: *Flag used by the Templars in battle.*

History

Rise

After Europeans in the First Crusade captured Jerusalem in 1099, many Christians made pilgrimages to various sacred sites in the Holy Land. Although the city of Jerusalem was relatively secure under Christian control, the rest of Outremer was not. Bandits and marauding highwaymen preyed upon pilgrims, who were routinely slaughtered, sometimes by the hundreds, as they attempted to make the journey from the coastline at Jaffa through to the interior of the Holy Land.[7]

In 1119, the French knight Hugues de Payens approached King Baldwin II of Jerusalem and Warmund, Patriarch of Jerusalem, and proposed creating a monastic order for the protection of these pilgrims. King Baldwin and Patriarch Warmund agreed to the request, probably at the Council of Nablus in January 1120, and the king granted the Templars a headquarters in a wing of the royal palace on the Temple Mount in the captured Al-Aqsa Mosque. The Temple Mount had a mystique because it was above what was believed to be the ruins of the Temple of Solomon.[8,9] The Crusaders therefore referred to the Al-Aqsa Mosque as Solomon's Temple, and from this location the new order took the name of *Poor Knights of Christ and the Temple of Solomon*, or "Templar" knights. The order, with about nine knights including Godfrey de Saint-Omer and André de Montbard, had few financial resources and relied on donations to survive. Their emblem was of two knights riding on a single horse, emphasising the order's poverty.[10]

Figure 2: *The first headquarters of the Knights Templar, on the Temple Mount in Jerusalem. The Crusaders called it "the Temple of Solomon" and from this location derived their name of Templar.*

The impoverished status of the Templars did not last long. They had a powerful advocate in Saint Bernard of Clairvaux, a leading Church figure, the French abbot primarily responsible for the founding of the Cistercian Order of monks and a nephew of André de Montbard, one of the founding knights. Bernard put his weight behind them and wrote persuasively on their behalf in the letter 'In Praise of the New Knighthood', and in 1129, at the Council of Troyes, he led a group of leading churchmen to officially approve and endorse the order on behalf of the church. With this formal blessing, the Templars became a favoured charity throughout Christendom, receiving money, land, businesses, and noble-born sons from families who were eager to help with the fight in the Holy Land. Another major benefit came in 1139, when Pope Innocent II's papal bull *Omne Datum Optimum* exempted the order from obedience to local laws. This ruling meant that the Templars could pass freely through all borders, were not required to pay any taxes, and were exempt from all authority except that of the pope.[11]

With its clear mission and ample resources, the order grew rapidly. Templars were often the advance shock troops in key battles of the Crusades, as the heavily armoured knights on their warhorses would set out to charge at the enemy, ahead of the main army bodies, in an attempt to break opposition lines. One of their most famous victories was in 1177 during the Battle of Montgisard, where some 500 Templar knights helped several thousand infantry to defeat Saladin's army of more than 26,000 soldiers.[12]

<templatestyles src="Template:Quote_box/styles.css" />

"A Templar Knight is truly a fearless knight, and secure on every side, for his soul is protected by the armour of faith, just as his body is protected by the armour of steel. He is thus doubly armed, and need fear neither demons nor men."

- —Bernard de Clairvaux, c. 1135,
- *De Laude Novae Militae – In Praise of the New Knighthood*

Although the primary mission of the order was militaristic, relatively few members were combatants. The others acted in support positions to assist the knights and to manage the financial infrastructure. The Templar Order, though its members were sworn to individual poverty, was given control of wealth beyond direct donations. A nobleman who was interested in participating in the Crusades might place all his assets under Templar management while he was away. Accumulating wealth in this manner throughout Christendom and the Outremer, the order in 1150 began generating letters of credit for pilgrims journeying to the Holy Land: pilgrims deposited their valuables with a local Templar preceptory before embarking, received a document indicating the value of their deposit, then used that document upon arrival in the Holy Land to retrieve their funds in an amount of treasure of equal value. This innovative arrangement was an early form of banking and may have been the first formal system to support the use of cheques; it improved the safety of pilgrims by making them less attractive targets for thieves, and also contributed to the Templar coffers.[13]

Based on this mix of donations and business dealing, the Templars established financial networks across the whole of Christendom. They acquired large tracts of land, both in Europe and the Middle East; they bought and managed farms and vineyards; they built massive stone cathedrals and castles; they were involved in manufacturing, import and export; they had their own fleet of ships; and at one point they even owned the entire island of Cyprus. The Order of the Knights Templar arguably qualifies as the world's first multinational corporation.

Decline

In the mid-12th century, the tide began to turn in the Crusades. The Muslim world had become more united under effective leaders such as Saladin, and dissension arose amongst Christian factions in, and concerning, the Holy Land. The Knights Templar were occasionally at odds with the two other

Figure 3: *Battle of Hattin in 1187, the turning point in the Crusades*

Christian military orders, the Knights Hospitaller and the Teutonic Knights, and decades of internecine feuds weakened Christian positions, both politically and militarily. After the Templars were involved in several unsuccessful campaigns, including the pivotal Battle of Hattin, Jerusalem was recaptured by Muslim forces under Saladin in 1187. The Holy Roman Emperor Frederick II reclaimed the city for Christians in the Sixth Crusade of 1229, without Templar aid, but only held it briefly for a little more than a decade. In 1244, the Ayyubid dynasty together with Khwarezmi mercenaries recaptured Jerusalem, and the city did not return to Western control until 1917 when, during World War I, the British captured it from the Ottoman Empire.[14]

The Templars were forced to relocate their headquarters to other cities in the north, such as the seaport of Acre, which they held for the next century. It was lost in 1291, followed by their last mainland strongholds, Tortosa (Tartus in what is now Syria) and Atlit in present-day Israel. Their headquarters then moved to Limassol on the island of Cyprus,[15] and they also attempted to maintain a garrison on tiny Arwad Island, just off the coast from Tortosa. In 1300, there was some attempt to engage in coordinated military efforts with the Mongols[16] via a new invasion force at Arwad. In 1302 or 1303, however, the Templars lost the island to the Egyptian Mamluk Sultanate in the Siege of Arwad. With the island gone, the Crusaders lost their last foothold in the Holy Land.

With the order's military mission now less important, support for the organization began to dwindle. The situation was complex, however, since during the two hundred years of their existence, the Templars had become a part of daily life throughout Christendom.[17] The organisation's Templar Houses, hundreds of which were dotted throughout Europe and the Near East, gave them a widespread presence at the local level. The Templars still managed many businesses, and many Europeans had daily contact with the Templar network, such as by working at a Templar farm or vineyard, or using the order as a bank in which to store personal valuables. The order was still not subject to local government, making it everywhere a "state within a state" – its standing army, though it no longer had a well-defined mission, could pass freely through all borders. This situation heightened tensions with some European nobility, especially as the Templars were indicating an interest in founding their own monastic state, just as the Teutonic Knights had done in Prussia[13] and the Knights Hospitaller were doing in Rhodes.[18]

Arrests, charges and dissolution

In 1305, the new Pope Clement V, based in Avignon, France, sent letters to both the Templar Grand Master Jacques de Molay and the Hospitaller Grand Master Fulk de Villaret to discuss the possibility of merging the two orders. Neither was amenable to the idea, but Pope Clement persisted, and in 1306 he invited both Grand Masters to France to discuss the matter. De Molay arrived first in early 1307, but de Villaret was delayed for several months. While waiting, De Molay and Clement discussed criminal charges that had been made two years earlier by an ousted Templar and were being discussed by King Philip IV of France and his ministers. It was generally agreed that the charges were false, but Clement sent the king a written request for assistance in the investigation. According to some historians, King Philip, who was already deeply in debt to the Templars from his war with the English, decided to seize upon the rumours for his own purposes. He began pressuring the church to take action against the order, as a way of freeing himself from his debts.[19]

At dawn on Friday, 13 October 1307 (a date sometimes linked with the origin of the Friday the 13th superstition) King Philip IV ordered de Molay and scores of other French Templars to be simultaneously arrested. The arrest warrant started with the phrase: "Dieu n'est pas content, nous avons des ennemis de la foi dans le Royaume" ["God is not pleased. We have enemies of the faith in the kingdom"]. Claims were made that during Templar admissions ceremonies, recruits were forced to spit on the Cross, deny Christ, and engage in indecent kissing; brethren were also accused of worshipping idols, and the order was said to have encouraged homosexual practices. The Templars were charged with numerous other offences such as financial corruption, fraud,

Figure 4: *Convent of Christ Castle in Tomar, Portugal. Built in 1160 as a stronghold for the Knights Templar, it became the headquarters of the renamed Order of Christ. In 1983, it was named a UNESCO World Heritage Site.*

and secrecy.[20] Many of the accused confessed to these charges under torture, and their confessions, even though obtained under duress, caused a scandal in Paris. The prisoners were coerced to confess that they had spat on the Cross: "Moi, Raymond de La Fère, 21 ans, reconnais que [j'ai] craché trois fois sur la Croix, mais de bouche et pas de cœur" (free translation: "I, Raymond de La Fère, 21 years old, admit that I have spat three times on the Cross, but only from my mouth and not from my heart"). The Templars were accused of idolatry and were suspected of worshiping either a figure known as Baphomet or a mummified severed head they recovered, amongst other artifacts, at their original headquarters on the Temple Mount that many scholars theorize might have been that of John the Baptist, among other things.

Relenting to Phillip's demands, Pope Clement then issued the papal bull *Pastoralis Praeeminentiae* on 22 November 1307, which instructed all Christian monarchs in Europe to arrest all Templars and seize their assets.[21] Pope Clement called for papal hearings to determine the Templars' guilt or innocence, and once freed of the Inquisitors' torture, many Templars recanted their confessions. Some had sufficient legal experience to defend themselves in the trials, but in 1310, having appointed the archbishop of Sens, Philippe de Marigny, to lead the investigation, Philip blocked this attempt, using the previously forced confessions to have dozens of Templars burned at the stake in

Figure 5: *Templars being burned at the stake.*

Paris.[22,23,24]

With Philip threatening military action unless the pope complied with his wishes, Pope Clement finally agreed to disband the order, citing the public scandal that had been generated by the confessions. At the Council of Vienne in 1312, he issued a series of papal bulls, including *Vox in excelso*, which officially dissolved the order, and *Ad providam*, which turned over most Templar assets to the Hospitallers.[25]

As for the leaders of the order, the elderly Grand Master Jacques de Molay, who had confessed under torture, retracted his confession. Geoffroi de Charney, Preceptor of Normandy, also retracted his confession and insisted on his innocence. Both men were declared guilty of being relapsed heretics, and they were sentenced to burn alive at the stake in Paris on 18 March 1314. De Molay reportedly remained defiant to the end, asking to be tied in such a way that he could face the Notre Dame Cathedral and hold his hands together in prayer.[26] According to legend, he called out from the flames that both Pope Clement and King Philip would soon meet him before God. His actual words were recorded on the parchment as follows : "Dieu sait qui a tort et a péché. Il va bientot arriver malheur à ceux qui nous ont condamnés à mort" (free translation : "God knows who is wrong and has sinned. Soon a calamity will occur to those who have condemned us to death"). Pope Clement died only a month later, and King Philip died in a hunting accident before the end of the year.[27,28,29]

With the last of the order's leaders gone, the remaining Templars around Europe were either arrested and tried under the Papal investigation (with virtually none convicted), absorbed into other military orders such as the Knights Hospitaller, or pensioned off and allowed to live out their days peacefully. By papal decree, the property of the Templars was transferred to the Knights Hospitaller, which also absorbed many of the Templars' members. In effect, the dissolution of the Templars could be seen as the merger of the two rival orders.[30] Templar organizations simply changed their name, from Knights Templar to *Order of Christ* and also a parallel *Supreme Order of Christ of the Holy See* in which both are considered the successors.[31,32]

Chinon Parchment

In September 2001, a document known as the "Chinon Parchment" dated 17–20 August 1308 was discovered in the Vatican Secret Archives by Barbara Frale, apparently after having been filed in the wrong place in 1628. It is a record of the trial of the Templars and shows that Clement absolved the Templars of all heresies in 1308 before formally disbanding the order in 1312, as did another Chinon Parchment dated 20 August 1308 addressed to Philip IV of France, also mentioning that all Templars that had confessed to heresy were "restored to the Sacraments and to the unity of the Church". This other Chinon Parchment has been well-known to historians,[33,34,35] having been published by Étienne Baluze in 1693[36] and by Pierre Dupuy in 1751.[37]

The current position of the Roman Catholic Church is that the medieval persecution of the Knights Templar was unjust, that nothing was inherently wrong with the order or its rule, and that Pope Clement was pressed into his actions by the magnitude of the public scandal and by the dominating influence of King Philip IV, who was Clement's relative.

Organization

The Templars were organized as a monastic order similar to Bernard's Cistercian Order, which was considered the first effective international organization in Europe.[38] The organizational structure had a strong chain of authority. Each country with a major Templar presence (France, Poitou, Anjou, Jerusalem, England, Aragon, Portugal, Italy, Tripoli, Antioch, Hungary, and Croatia)[39] had a Master of the Order for the Templars in that region.

All of them were subject to the Grand Master, appointed for life, who oversaw both the order's military efforts in the East and their financial holdings in the

Figure 6: *Templar chapel from the 12th century in Metz, France. Once part of the Templar commandery of Metz, the oldest Templar institution of the Holy Roman Empire.*

West. The Grand Master exercised his authority via the visitors-general of the order, who were knights specially appointed by the Grand Master and convent of Jerusalem to visit the different provinces, correct malpractices, introduce new regulations, and resolve important disputes. The visitors-general had the power to remove knights from office and to suspend the Master of the province concerned.

No precise numbers exist, but it is estimated that at the order's peak there were between 15,000 and 20,000 Templars, of whom about a tenth were actual knights.[1]

Figure 7: *Templar building at Saint Martin des Champs, France*

Ranks within the order

Three main ranks

There was a threefold division of the ranks of the Templars: the noble knights, the non-noble sergeants, and the chaplains. The Templars did not perform knighting ceremonies, so any knight wishing to become a Knight Templar had to be a knight already. They were the most visible branch of the order, and wore the famous white mantles to symbolize their purity and chastity. They were equipped as heavy cavalry, with three or four horses and one or two squires. Squires were generally not members of the order but were instead outsiders who were hired for a set period of time. Beneath the knights in the order and drawn from non-noble families were the sergeants.[40] They brought vital skills and trades from blacksmiths and builders, including administration of many of the order's European properties. In the Crusader States, they fought alongside the knights as light cavalry with a single horse.[41] Several of the order's most senior positions were reserved for sergeants, including the post of Commander of the Vault of Acre, who was the *de facto* Admiral of the Templar fleet. The sergeants wore black or brown. From 1139, chaplains constituted a third Templar class. They were ordained priests who cared for the Templars' spiritual needs.[30] All three classes of brother wore the order's red cross.

Grand Masters

Starting with founder Hugues de Payens in 1118–1119, the order's highest office was that of Grand Master, a position which was held for life, though considering the martial nature of the order, this could mean a very short tenure. All but two of the Grand Masters died in office, and several died during military campaigns. For example, during the Siege of Ascalon in 1153, Grand Master Bernard de Tremelay led a group of 40 Templars through a breach in the city walls. When the rest of the Crusader army did not follow, the Templars, including their Grand Master, were surrounded and beheaded.[42] Grand Master Gérard de Ridefort was beheaded by Saladin in 1189 at the Siege of Acre.

The Grand Master oversaw all of the operations of the order, including both the military operations in the Holy Land and Eastern Europe and the Templars' financial and business dealings in Western Europe. Some Grand Masters also served as battlefield commanders, though this was not always wise: several blunders in de Ridefort's combat leadership contributed to the devastating defeat at the Battle of Hattin. The last Grand Master was Jacques de Molay, burned at the stake in Paris in 1314 by order of King Philip IV.[24]

Behaviour, clothing and beards

Bernard de Clairvaux and founder Hugues de Payens devised the specific code of behavior for the Templar Order, known to modern historians as the Latin Rule. Its 72 clauses defined the ideal behavior for the Knights, such as the types of garments they were to wear and how many horses they could have. Knights were to take their meals in silence, eat meat no more than three times per week, and not have physical contact of any kind with women, even members of their own family. A Master of the Order was assigned "4 horses, and one chaplain-brother and one clerk with three horses, and one sergeant brother with two horses, and one gentleman valet to carry his shield and lance, with one horse."[43] As the order grew, more guidelines were added, and the original list of 72 clauses was expanded to several hundred in its final form.[44,45]

The knights wore a white surcoat with a red cross and a white mantle also with a red cross; the sergeants wore a black tunic with a red cross on the front and a black or brown mantle.[46,47] The white mantle was assigned to the Templars at the Council of Troyes in 1129, and the cross was most probably added to their robes at the launch of the Second Crusade in 1147, when Pope Eugenius III, King Louis VII of France, and many other notables attended a meeting of the French Templars at their headquarters near Paris.[48] According to their Rule, the knights were to wear the white mantle at all times, even being forbidden to eat or drink unless they were wearing it.[49]

Figure 8: *Representation of a Knight Templar (Ten Duinen Abbey museum, 2010 photograph)*

The red cross that the Templars wore on their robes was a symbol of martyrdom, and to die in combat was considered a great honour that assured a place in heaven.[50] There was a cardinal rule that the warriors of the order should never surrender unless the Templar flag had fallen, and even then they were first to try to regroup with another of the Christian orders, such as that of the Hospitallers. Only after all flags had fallen were they allowed to leave the battlefield.[51]

Although not prescribed by the Templar Rule, it later became customary for members of the order to wear long and prominent beards. In about 1240, Alberic of Trois-Fontaines described the Templars as an "order of bearded brethren"; while during the interrogations by the papal commissioners in Paris in 1310–1311, out of nearly 230 knights and brothers questioned, 76 are described as wearing a beard, in some cases specified as being "in the style of the Templars", and 133 are said to have shaved off their beards, either in renunciation of the order or because they had hoped to escape detection.[52]

Initiation,[53] known as Reception (*receptio*) into the order, was a profound commitment and involved a solemn ceremony. Outsiders were discouraged from attending the ceremony, which aroused the suspicions of medieval inquisitors during the later trials. New members had to willingly sign over all of

Figure 9: *Depiction of two Templars seated on a horse (emphasising poverty), with Beauséant, the "sacred banner" (or gonfanon) of the Templars, argent a chief sable (Matthew Paris, c. 1250).*

their wealth and goods to the order and take vows of poverty, chastity, piety, and obedience. Most brothers joined for life, although some were allowed to join for a set period. Sometimes a married man was allowed to join if he had his wife's permission,[47] but he was not allowed to wear the white mantle.[54]

Legacy

With their military mission and extensive financial resources, the Knights Templar funded a large number of building projects around Europe and the Holy Land. Many of these structures are still standing. Many sites also maintain the name "Temple" because of centuries-old association with the Templars.[55] For example, some of the Templars' lands in London were later rented to lawyers, which led to the names of the Temple Bar gateway and the Temple Underground station. Two of the four Inns of Court which may call members to act as barristers are the Inner Temple and Middle Temple – the entire area known as Temple, London.

Distinctive architectural elements of Templar buildings include the use of the image of "two knights on a single horse", representing the Knights' poverty,

Figure 10: *Temple Church, London. As the chapel of the New Temple in London, it was the location for Templar initiation ceremonies. In modern times it is the parish church of the Middle and Inner Temples, two of the Inns of Court, and a popular tourist attraction.*

and round buildings designed to resemble the Church of the Holy Sepulchre in Jerusalem.[56]

Modern organizations

The story of the persecution and sudden dissolution of the secretive yet powerful medieval Templars has drawn many other groups to use alleged connections with them as a way of enhancing their own image and mystery. The Knights Templar were dismantled in the Rolls of the Catholic Church in 1309 with the death of Jacques de Molay; there is no clear historical connection between them and any modern organization, the earliest of which emerged publicly in the 18th century.[57,58,59,60]

Temperance movement

Many temperance organizations named themselves after the Poor Fellow-Soldiers of Christ and of the Temple of Solomon, citing the belief that the original Knights Templar "drank sour milk, and also because they were fighting 'a great crusade' against 'this terrible vice' of alcohol." The largest of these, the International Order of Good Templars (IOGT), grew throughout the world after being started in the 19th century and continues to advocate for the abstinence of alcohol and other drugs.

Freemasonry

Freemasonry has incorporated the symbols and rituals of several medieval military orders in a number of Masonic bodies since the 18th century at least. This can be seen in the "Red Cross of Constantine," inspired by the Military Constantinian Order; the "Order of Malta," inspired by the Knights Hospitaller; and the "Order of the Temple", inspired by the Knights Templar. The Orders of Malta and the Temple feature prominently in the York Rite. One theory on the origin of Freemasonry claims direct descent from the historical Knights Templar through its final fourteenth-century members who allegedly took refuge in Scotland and aided Robert the Bruce in his victory at Bannockburn. This theory is usually rejected by both Masonic authorities[61] and historians due to lack of evidence.

Modern popular culture

The Knights Templar have become associated with legends concerning secrets and mysteries handed down to the select from ancient times. Rumours circulated even during the time of the Templars themselves. Masonic writers added their own speculations in the 18th century, and further fictional embellishments have been added in popular novels such as *Ivanhoe*, *Foucault's Pendulum*, and *The Da Vinci Code*, modern movies such as *National Treasure*, *The Last Templar*, and *Indiana Jones and the Last Crusade*, as well as video games such as *Broken Sword* and *Assassin's Creed*.

Beginning in the 1960s, there have been speculative popular publications surrounding the order's early occupation of the Temple Mount in Jerusalem and speculation about what relics the Templars may have found there, such as the Holy Grail or the Ark of the Covenant,[62] or the historical accusation of idol worship (Baphomet) transformed into a context of "witchcraft".

The association of the Holy Grail with the Templars has precedents even in 12th century fiction; Wolfram von Eschenbach's *Parzival* calls the knights guarding the Grail Kingdom *templeisen*, apparently a conscious fictionalisation of the *templarii*.[63]

References

Notes

Bibliography <templatestyles src="Template:Refbegin/styles.css" />
- Isle of Avalon, Lundy. " The Rule of the Knights Templar A Powerful Champion[64]" The Knights Templar. Mystic Realms, 2010. Web. 30 May 2010.
- Barber, Malcolm (1994). *The New Knighthood: A History of the Order of the Temple*. Cambridge: Cambridge University Press. ISBN 0-521-42041-5.
- Barber, Malcolm (1993). *The Trial of the Templars* (1 ed.). Cambridge: Cambridge University Press. ISBN 0-521-45727-0.
- Barber, Malcolm (2006). *The Trial of the Templars* (2 ed.). Cambridge: Cambridge University Press. ISBN 978-0-521-67236-8.
- Barber, Malcolm (1992). "Supplying the Crusader States: The Role of the Templars". In Benjamin Z. Kedar. *The Horns of Hattin*. Jerusalem and London. pp. 314–326.
- Barrett, Jim (1996). "Science and the Shroud: Microbiology meets archaeology in a renewed quest for answers"[65]. *The Mission*. University of Texas Health Science Center (Spring). Retrieved 2008-12-25.
- Burman, Edward (1990). *The Templars: Knights of God*. Rochester: Destiny Books. ISBN 0-89281-221-4.
- Mario Dal Bello, *Gli Ultimi Giorni dei Templari,* Città Nuova, 2013, ean 9788831164511
- Frale, Barbara (2004). "The Chinon chart – Papal absolution to the last Templar, Master Jacques de Molay". *Journal of Medieval History*. **30** (2): 109. doi: 10.1016/j.jmedhist.2004.03.004[66].
- Hietala, Heikki (1996). "The Knights Templar: Serving God with the Sword"[67]. *Renaissance Magazine*. Archived from the original[68] on 2 October 2008. Retrieved 2008-12-26.
- Marcy Marzuni (2005). *Decoding the Past: The Templar Code*[69] (Video documentary). The History Channel.
- Stuart Elliott (2006). *Lost Worlds: Knights Templar* (Video documentary). The History Channel.
- Martin, Sean (2005). *The Knights Templar: The History & Myths of the Legendary Military Order*. New York: Thunder's Mouth Press. ISBN 1-56025-645-1.
- ⓘ Moeller, Charles (1912). "Knights Templars". In Herbermann, Charles. *Catholic Encyclopedia*. **14**. New York: Robert Appleton Company.
- Newman, Sharan (2007). *The Real History behind the Templars*. New York: Berkley Trade. ISBN 978-0-425-21533-3.

- Nicholson, Helen (2001). *The Knights Templar: A New History*. Stroud: Sutton. ISBN 0-7509-2517-5.
- Picknett, Lynn; Clive Prince (1998). *The Templar Revelation*. New York: Touchstone. ISBN 0-684-84891-0.
- Read, Piers (2001). *The Templars*. New York: Da Capo Press. ISBN 0-306-81071-9.
- Selwood, Dominic (2002). *Knights of the Cloister. Templars and Hospitallers in Central-Southern Occitania 1100–1300*. Woodbridge: The Boydell Press. ISBN 0851158285.
- Selwood, Dominic (1996). *'Quidam autem dubitaverunt: the Saint, the Sinner. and a Possible Chronology' in Autour de la Première Croisade,*. Paris: Publications de la Sorbonne. ISBN 2859443088.
- Selwood, Dominic. " The Knights Templar 1: The Knights[70] (2013)
- Selwood, Dominic. " The Knights Templar 2: Sergeants, Women, Chaplains, Affiliates[71] (2013)
- Selwood, Dominic. " The Knights Templar 3: Birth of the Order[72] (2013)
- Selwood, Dominic. " The Knights Templar 4: Saint Bernard of Clairvaux[73] (2013)
- Sobecki, Sebastian (2006). "MARIGNY, Philippe de"[74]. *Biographisch-bibliographisches Kirchenlexikon* (26 ed.). Bautz: Nordhausen. p. 963-64.
- Julien Théry, "Philip the Fair, the Trial of the 'Perfidious Templars' and the Pontificalization of the French Monarchy", in *Journal of Medieval Religious Culture*, 39/2 (2013), pp. 117–148, online[75]

Further reading

<templatestyles src="Template:Refbegin/styles.css" />

- Malcolm Barber, Keith Bate. *The Templars: Selected sources translated and annotated by Malcolm Barber and Keith Bate* (Manchester University Press, 2002) ISBN 0-7190-5110-X
- Addison, Charles. *The History of the Knights Templar*[76] (1842)
- d'Albon, André. *Cartulaire général de l'ordre du Temple: 1119?–1150*[77] *(1913–1922) (at Gallica)*
- Barber, Malcolm (2006-04-20). "The Knights Templar – Who were they? And why do we care?"[78]. *Slate Magazine*. ;
- Brighton, Simon (2006-06-15). *In Search of the Knights Templar: A Guide to the Sites in Britain*. London, England: Orion Publishing Group. ISBN 0-297-84433-4.
- Butler, Alan; Stephen Dafoe (1998). *The Warriors and the Bankers: A History of the Knights Templar from 1307 to the present*. Belleville: Templar Books. ISBN 0-9683567-2-9.

- ⓦ Chisholm, Hugh, ed. (1911). "Templars". *Encyclopædia Britannica*. **26** (11th ed.). Cambridge University Press.
- Frale, Barbara (2009). *The Templars: The secret history revealed*. Dunboyne: Maverick House Publishers. ISBN 978-1-905379-60-6.
- Gordon, Franck (2012). *The Templar Code: French title: Le Code Templier*. Paris, France: Yvelinedition. ISBN 978-2-84668-253-4.
- Haag, Michael (2012). *The Tragedy of the Templars*. London: Profile Books Ltd. ISBN 978-1-84668-450-0.
- Haag, Michael (2008). *The Templars: History and Myth*. London: Profile Books Ltd. ISBN 978-1-84668-148-6.
- Hodapp, Christopher; Alice Von Kannon (2007). *The Templar Code For Dummies*. Hoboken, NJ: Wiley. ISBN 0-470-12765-1.
- Levaye, Patrick. Géopolitique du Catholicisme (Éditions Ellipses, 2007) ISBN 2-7298-3523-7
- Partner, Peter (1990). *The Knights Templar & Their Myth*. Rochester: Destiny Books. ISBN 0-89281-273-7.
- Ralls, Karen (2003). *The Templars and the Grail*. Wheaton: Quest Books. ISBN 0-8356-0807-7.
- Smart, George (2005). *The Knights Templar Chronology*. Bloomington: Authorhouse. ISBN 1-4184-9889-0.
- Upton-Ward, Judith Mary (1992). *The Rule of the Templars: The French Text of the Rule of the Order of the Knights Templar*. Ipswich: Boydell Press. ISBN 0-85115-315-1.

External links

 Wikimedia Commons has media related to *Knights Templar*.

- Knights Templar[79] at Curlie (based on DMOZ)

<indicator name="featured-star"> ⭐ </indicator>

History

History of the Knights Templar

The Crusades and the Knights Templar

The Knights Templar were the elite fighting force of their day, highly trained, well-equipped and highly motivated; one of the tenets of their religious order was that they were forbidden from retreating in battle, unless outnumbered three to one, and even then only by order of their commander, or if the Templar flag went down. Not all Knights Templar were warriors. The mission of most of the members was one of support – to acquire resources which could be used to fund and equip the small percentage of members who were fighting on the front lines. There were actually three classes within the orders. The highest class was the knight. When a candidate was sworn into the order, the initiation made the knight a monk. They wore white robes. The knights could hold no property and receive no private letters. He could not be married or betrothed and cannot have any vow in any other Order. He could not have debt more than he could pay, and no infirmities. The Templar priest class was similar to the modern day military chaplain. Wearing green robes, they conducted religious services, led prayers, and were assigned record keeping and letter writing. They always wore gloves, unless they were giving Holy Communion. The mounted men-at-arms represented the most common class, and they were called "brothers". They were usually assigned two horses each and held many positions, including guard, steward, squire or other support vocations. As the main support staff, they wore black or brown robes and were partially garbed in chain mail or plate mail. The armor was not as complete as the knights. Because of this infrastructure, the warriors were well-trained and very well armed. Even their horses were trained to fight in combat, fully armored.[80] The combination of soldier and monk was also a powerful one, as to the Templar knights, martyrdom in battle was one of the most glorious ways to die.

Figure 11: *Two Templars burned at the stake, including Jacques de Molay, from a French 15th-century manuscript*

The Templars were also shrewd tacticians, following the dream of Saint Bernard who had declared that a small force, under the right conditions, could defeat a much larger enemy. One of the key battles in which this was demonstrated was in 1177, at the Battle of Montgisard. The famous Muslim military leader Saladin was attempting to push toward Jerusalem from the south, with a force of 26,000 soldiers. He had pinned the forces of Jerusalem's King Baldwin IV, about 500 knights and their supporters, near the coast, at Ascalon. Eighty Templar knights and their own entourage attempted to reinforce. They met Saladin's troops at Gaza, but were considered too small a force to be worth fighting, so Saladin turned his back on them and headed with his army towards Jerusalem.

Once Saladin and his army had moved on, the Templars were able to join King Baldwin's forces, and together they proceeded north along the coast. Saladin had made a key mistake at that point – instead of keeping his forces together, he permitted his army to temporarily spread out and pillage various villages on their way to Jerusalem. The Templars took advantage of this low state of readiness to launch a surprise ambush directly against Saladin and his bodyguard, at Montgisard near Ramla. Saladin's army was spread too thin to adequately defend themselves, and he and his forces were forced to fight a losing battle as they retreated back to the south, ending up with only a tenth of their original number. The battle was not the final one with Saladin, but it bought a year of peace for the Kingdom of Jerusalem, and the victory became a heroic legend.

Another key tactic of the Templars was that of the "squadron charge". A small group of knights and their heavily armed warhorses would gather into a tight unit which would gallop full speed at the enemy lines, with a determination and force of will that made it clear that they would rather commit suicide than fall back. This terrifying onslaught would frequently have the desired result of breaking a hole in the enemy lines, thereby giving the other Crusader forces an advantage.[81]

The Templars, though relatively small in number, routinely joined other armies in key battles. They would be the force that would ram through the enemy's front lines at the beginning of a battle, or the fighters that would protect the army from the rear. They fought alongside King Louis VII of France, and King Richard I of England.[82] In addition to battles in Palestine, members of the Order also fought in the Spanish and Portuguese *Reconquista*.

Bankers

Though initially an Order of poor monks, the official papal sanction made the Knights Templar a charity across Europe. Further resources came in when members joined the Order, as they had to take oaths of poverty, and therefore often donated large amounts of their original cash or property to the Order. Additional revenue came from business dealings. Since the monks themselves were sworn to poverty, but had the strength of a large and trusted international infrastructure behind them, nobles would occasionally use them as a kind of bank or power of attorney. If a noble wished to join the Crusades, this might entail an absence of years from their home. So some nobles would place all of their wealth and businesses under the control of Templars, to safeguard it for them until their return. The Order's financial power became substantial, and the majority of the Order's infrastructure was devoted not to combat, but to economic pursuits.

By 1150, the Order's original mission of guarding pilgrims had changed into a mission of guarding their valuables through an innovative way of issuing letters of credit, an early precursor of modern banking. Pilgrims would visit a Templar house in their home country, depositing their deeds and valuables. The Templars would then give them a letter which would describe their holdings. Modern scholars have stated that the letters were encrypted with a cipher alphabet based on a Maltese Cross; however there is some disagreement on this, and it is possible that the code system was introduced later, and not something used by the medieval Templars themselves.[83] While traveling, the pilgrims could present the letter to other Templars along the way, to "withdraw" funds

Figure 12: *Knights Templar playing chess, 1283*

from their accounts. This kept the pilgrims safe since they were not carrying valuables, and further increased the power of the Templars.

The Knights' involvement in banking grew over time into a new basis for money, as Templars became increasingly involved in banking activities. One indication of their powerful political connections is that the Templars' involvement in usury did not lead to more controversy within the Order and the church at large. Officially the idea of lending money in return for interest was forbidden by the church, but the Order sidestepped this with clever loopholes, such as a stipulation that the Templars retained the rights to the production of mortgaged property. Or as one Templar researcher put it, "Since they weren't allowed to charge interest, they charged rent instead."[84]

Their holdings were necessary to support their campaigns; in 1180, a Burgundian noble required 3 square kilometres of estate to support himself as a knight, and by 1260 this had risen to 15.6 km². The Order potentially supported up to 4,000 horses and pack animals at any given time, if provisions of the rule were followed; these horses had extremely high maintenance costs due to the heat in *Outremer* (Crusader states at the Eastern Mediterranean), and had high mortality rates due to both disease and the Turkish bowmen strategy of aiming at a knight's horse rather than the knight himself. In addition, the high mortality rates of the knights in the East (regularly ninety percent in battle, not including wounded) resulted in extremely high campaign costs due to the need to recruit and train more knights. In 1244, at the battle of La Forbie, where only thirty-three of 300 knights survived, it is estimated the financial loss was equivalent to one-ninth of the entire Capetian yearly revenue.Wikipedia:Citation needed

History of the Knights Templar

Figure 13: *The Battle of Hattin*

The Templars' political connections and awareness of the essentially urban and commercial nature of the *Outremer* communities led the Order to a position of significant power, both in Europe and the Holy Land.Wikipedia:Citation needed They owned large tracts of land both in Europe and the Middle East, built churches and castles, bought farms and vineyards, were involved in manufacturing and import/export, had their own fleet of ships, and for a time even "owned" the entire island of Cyprus.[85]

Decline

Their success attracted the concern of many other orders, with the two most powerful rivals being the Knights Hospitaller and the Teutonic Knights. Various nobles also had concerns about the Templars as well, both for financial reasons, and nervousness about an independent army that was able to move freely through all borders.

The long-famed military acumen of the Templars began to stumble in the 1180s. On July 4, 1187, came the disastrous Battle of the Horns of Hattin, a turning point in the Crusades. It again involved Saladin, who had been beaten back by the Templars in 1177 in the legendary Battle of Montgisard near Tiberias, but this time Saladin was better prepared. Further, the Grand Master of the Templars was involved in this battle, Gerard de Ridefort, who had just achieved that lifetime position a few years earlier. He was not known as a good military strategist, and made some deadly errors, such as venturing out with his force of 80 knights without adequate supplies or water, across the arid hill country of Galilee. The Templars were overcome by the heat within a day, and then surrounded and massacred by Saladin's army. Within months Saladin captured Jerusalem.

But in the early 1190s, in a remarkably short and powerfully effective campaign, Richard the Lionheart, King of England and leader of the Third Crusade, together with his allies the Templars, delivered a series of powerful blows against Saladin and recovered much of Christian territory. In name and number the revived Crusader states were as before, but their outlines were diminished. There was the Kingdom of Jerusalem, though its capital was at Acre, which the Templars made their new headquarters. To the north was the County of Tripoli. But the Muslims retained control of the Syrian coast around Latakia for some time, and so the Principality of Antioch further to the north was now no longer contiguous to the other Crusader states. Nevertheless, the Third Crusade, in which Richard relied heavily on the Templars, had saved the Holy Land for the Christians and went a long way towards restoring Frankish fortunes. In this he was abetted by the military orders, whose great castles stood like islands of Frankish power amid the Muslim torrent. More than ever the Crusader states were relying on the military orders in their castles and on the field of battle, and the power of the orders grew. In fact at no point in their history would the Templars be more powerful than in the century to come.

But after the Siege of Acre in 1291, the Templars were forced to relocate their headquarters to the island of Cyprus.

Jacques de Molay, who was to be the last of the Order's Grand Masters, took office around 1292. One of his first tasks was to tour across Europe, to raise support for the Order and try to organise another Crusade. He met the newly invested Pope Boniface VIII, who agreed to grant the Templars the same privileges at Cyprus as they had held in the Holy Land. Charles II of Naples and Edward I also pledged varying types of support, either continuing to exempt the Templars from taxes, or pledging future support towards building a new army.[86]

Final attempts to regain the Holy Land (1298–1300)

In 1298 or 1299, the military orders (the Knights Templar and Knights Hospitaller) and their leaders, including Jacques de Molay, Otton de Grandson and the Great Master of the Hospitallers, briefly campaigned in Armenia, in order to fight off an invasion by the Mamluks. They were not successful and soon the fortress of Roche-Guillaume in the Belen Pass, the last Templar stronghold in Antioch, was lost to the Muslims.

In 1300, the Templars, along with the Knights Hospitaller and forces from Cyprus attempted to retake the coastal city of Tortosa. They were able to take the island of Arwad, near Tortosa, but lost it soon after. With the loss of Arwad, the Crusaders had lost their last foothold in the Holy Land.[87]

Though they still had a base of operations in Cyprus, and controlled considerable financial resources, the Order of the Templars became an Order without a clear purpose or support, but which still had enormous financial power. This unstable situation contributed to their downfall.

Fall

King Philip had other reasons to mistrust the Templars, as the organization had declared its desire to form its own state, similar to how the Teutonic Knights had founded Prussia. The Templars' preferred location for this was in the Languedoc of southeastern France,Wikipedia:Citation needed but they had also made a plan for the island of Cyprus. In 1306, the Templars had supported a coup on that island, which had forced King Henry II of Cyprus to abdicate his throne in favor of his brother, Amalric of Tyre. This probably made Philip particularly uneasy, since just a few years earlier he had inherited land in the region of Champagne, France, which was the Templars' headquarters. The Templars were already a "state within a state", were institutionally wealthy, paid no taxes, and had a large standing army which by papal decree could move freely through all European borders. However, this army no longer had a presence in the Holy Land, leaving it with no battlefield. These factors, plus the fact that Philip had inherited an impoverished kingdom from his father and was already deeply in debt to the Templars, were probably what led to his actions. However, recent studies emphasize the political and religious motivations of the French king. It seems that, with the "discovery" and repression of the "Templars' heresy," the Capetian monarchy claimed for itself the mystic foundations of the papal theocracy. The Temple case was the last step of a process of appropriating these foundations, which had begun with the Franco-papal rift at the time of Boniface VIII. Being the ultimate defender of the Catholic faith, the Capetian king was invested with a Christlike function that put him above the pope : what was at stake in the Templars' trial, then, was the establishment of a "royal theocracy".[88]

At dawn on Friday, October 13, 1307, scores of French Templars were simultaneously arrested by agents of King Philip, later to be tortured in locations such as the tower at Chinon, into admitting heresy and other sacrilegious offenses in the Order. Then they were put to death. There were five initial charges lodged against the Templars. The first was the renouncement and spitting on the cross during initiation into the Order. The second was the stripping of the man to be initiated and the thrice kissing of that man by the preceptor on the navel, posteriors and the mouth. The third was telling the neophyte (novice) that unnatural lust was lawful and indulged in commonly. The fourth was that the cord worn by the neophyte day and night was consecrated by wrapping it around an idol in the form of a human head with a great beard, and that this idol was adored in all chapters. The fifth was that the priests of the order did not consecrate the host in celebrating Mass.[89,90] On August 12, 1308, the charges would be increased and would become more outrageous, one specifically stated that the Templars worshipped idols, specifically made of a cat and a head, the latter having three faces. The lists of articles 86 to 127[3] would add many other charges.[91,92] The majority of these charges were identical to the charges that had been earlier issued against the inconvenient Pope Boniface VIII: accusations of denying Christ, spitting and urinating on the cross, and devil worship. Of the 138 Templars (many of them old men) questioned in Paris over the next few years, 105 of them "confessed" to denying Christ during the secret Templar initiations. 103 confessed to an "obscene kiss" being part of the ceremonies, and 123 said they spat on the cross. Throughout the trial there was never any physical evidence of wrongdoing, and no independent witnesses; the only "proof" was obtained through confessions induced by torture. The Templars reached out to the Pope for assistance, and Pope Clement did write letters to King Philip questioning the arrests, but took no further action.

Despite the fact that the confessions had been produced under duress, they caused a scandal in Paris, with mobs calling for action against the blaspheming Order. In response to this public pressure, along with more bullying from King Philip, Pope Clement issued the bull *Pastoralis Praeeminentiae*, which instructed all Christian monarchs in Europe to arrest all Templars and seize their assets.[93] Most monarchs simply didn't believe the charges, though proceedings were started in England, Iberia, Germany, Italy, and Cyprus,[94] with the likelihood of a confession being dependent on whether or not torture was used to extract it.

The dominant view is that Philip, who seized the treasury and broke up the monastic banking system, was jealous of the Templars' wealth and power, and frustrated by his enormous debt to them, sought to seize their financial resources for himself by bringing blatantly false charges against them at the Tours assembly in 1308. It is almost impossible to believe, that, under the influence of his carefully chosen advisors (the same that had persecuted Boniface), he actually believed the charges to be true. It is widely accepted that Philip had clearly made up the accusations, some nearly identical to those made against Boniface, and did not believe any of the Templars to have been party to such activities. It is a fact that he had invited Jacques de Molay to be a pall-bearer at the funeral of the King's sister on the very day before the arrests.[95]

Figure 14: *Pope Clement V*

The arrests caused some shifts in the European economy, from a system of military fiat back to European money, removing this power from Church orders. Seeing the fate of the Templars, the Hospitallers of St John of Jerusalem and of Rhodes were also convinced to give up banking at this time.

Dismantling

In 1312, after the Council of Vienne, and under extreme pressure from King Philip IV, Pope Clement V issued an edict officially dissolving the Order. Many kings and nobles who had been supporting the Knights up until that time, finally acquiesced and dissolved the orders in their fiefs in accordance with the Papal command. Most were not so brutal as the French. In England, many Knights were arrested and tried, but not found guilty.

Much of the Templar property outside France was transferred by the Pope to the Knights Hospitaller, and many surviving Templars were also accepted into the Hospitallers. In the Iberian Peninsula, where the king of Aragon was against giving the heritage of the Templars to the Hospitallers (as commanded by Clement V), the Order of Montesa took Templar assets.

The order continued to exist in Portugal, simply changing its name to the Order of Christ. This group was believed to have contributed to the first naval discoveries of the Portuguese. Prince Henry the Navigator led the Portuguese order for 20 years until the time of his death.

Even with the absorption of Templars into other Orders, there are still questions as to what became of all of the tens of thousands of Templars across Europe. There had been 15,000 "Templar Houses", and an entire fleet of ships. Even in France where hundreds of Templars had been rounded up and arrested, this was only a small percentage of the estimated 3,000 Templars in the entire country. Also, the extensive archive of the Templars, with detailed records of all of their business holdings and financial transactions, was never found. By papal bull it was to have been transferred to the Hospitallers.

A popular thread of conspiracy theory originating with Holy Blood, Holy Grail has it that the Templars used a fleet of 18 ships at La Rochelle to escape arrest in France. The fleet allegedly left laden with knights and treasures just before the issue of the warrant for the arrest of the Order in October 1307. This, in turn, was based on a single item of testimony from serving brother Jean de Châlon, who says he had "heard people talking that [Gerard de Villiers had] put to sea with 18 galleys, and the brother Hugues de Chalon fled with the whole treasury of the brother Hugues de Pairaud." However, aside from being the sole source for this statement, the transcript indicates that it is hearsay, and this serving brother seems to be prone to making some of the wildest and most damning of claims about the Order, which have led some to doubt his credibility.

In *Holy Blood, Holy Grail,* the knights that allegedly boarded these ships then escaped to Scotland, but in some versions the Templars are even claimed to have left for North America, burying a treasure in Oak Island, Nova Scotia, Canada (a story taken up in the 2004 movie *National Treasure* starring Nicolas Cage). However, many historians have questioned the plausibility of this scenario. For example, historian Helen Nicholson has argued that

> The Templars did have ships to carry personnel, pilgrims and supplies across the Mediterranean between the West and East and back, but if the Hospital after 1312 is any guide they did not have more than four galleys (warships) and few other ships, and if they needed more they hired them. They certainly could not spare ships to indulge in world exploration ... [T]he records of the port of La Rochelle show that the Templars were exporting wine by ship. This was not a fleet in any modern sense: again, those would have been transport vessels rather than warships, and the Templars probably hired them as they needed them, rather than buying their own. ... The ships would have been very small by modern standards, too shallow in draught and sailing too low in the water to be able to withstand the heavy waves and winds of the open Atlantic, and suited for use only in the relatively shallow waters of the continental shelf. What was more, they could not carry enough water to be at sea for long periods.

Nicholson's argument, however, is an assessment of the fleet in 1312 - according to the LaRochelle Theory, many ships would already have disappeared bound for many of the aforementioned destinations and stands to reason their fleet would seem depleted in the following years after the arrest of the Templars.

Heresy, blasphemy, and other charges

There were five initial charges lodged against the Templars. The first was the renouncement and spitting on the cross during initiation into the Order. The second was the stripping of the man to be initiated and the thrice kissing of that man by the preceptor on the navel, posteriors and the mouth. The third was telling the neophyte (novice) that unnatural lust was lawful and indulged in commonly. The fourth was that the cord worn by the neophyte day and night was consecrated by wrapping it around an idol in the form of a human head with a great beard, and that this idol was adored in all chapters. The fifth was that the priests of the order did not consecrate the host in celebrating Mass. Subsequently, the charges would be increased and would become, according to the procedures, lists of articles 86 to 127[3] in which will be added a few other charges, such as the prohibition to priests who do not belong to the order.

The incontrovertibility of the evidence that the Templar priests did not mutilate the words of consecration in the mass is furnished in the Cypriote proceedings by ecclesiastics who had long dwelt with them in the East.[96]

Debate continues as to whether the accusation of religious heresy had merit by the standards of the time. Under torture, some Templars admitted to sodomy and to the worship of heads and an idol known as *Baphomet*. Their leaders later denied these admissions, and for that were executed. Some scholars, such as Malcolm Barber, Helen Nicholson and Peter Partner, discount these as forced admissions, typical during the Medieval Inquisition.

The majority of the charges were identical to other people being tortured by the Inquisitors, with one exception: head worship. The Templars were specifically charged with worshipping some type of severed head; a charge which was made only against Templars. The descriptions of the head allegedly venerated by the Templars were varied and contradictory in nature. Quoting Norman Cohn:

> *Some describe it as having three faces, others as having four feet, others as being simply a face with no feet. For some it was a human skull, embalmed and encrusted with jewels; for others it was carved out of wood. Some maintained that it came from the remains of a former grand master of the order, while others were equally convinced that it was Baphomet – which in turn was interpreted as 'Mohammed'. Some saw it as having horns.*[97]

Figure 15: *The manuscript illustration (c. 1350) alludes to the accusation of "obscene kisses" at the base of the spine*

Barber has linked this charge to medieval folklore about magical heads, and the popular medieval belief that the Muslims worshipped idols.[98] Some argue it referred to rituals involving the alleged relics of John the Baptist,[99] Euphemia,[100] one of Ursula's eleven maidens,[101] and/or Hugues de Payens[102] rather than pagan idols.

The charges of heresy included *spitting, trampling, or urinating on the cross*; while naked, being *kissed obscenely by the receptor on the lips, navel, and base of the spine*; *heresy and worship of idols*; *institutionalized sodomy*; and also accusations of *contempt of the Holy Mass and denial of the sacraments*. Barbara Frale has suggested that these acts were intended to simulate the kind of humiliation and torture that a Crusader might be subjected to if captured by the Saracens. According to this line of reasoning, they were taught how to commit apostasy *with the mind only and not with the heart*.[103]

The accusation of venerating *Baphomet* is more problematic. Karen Ralls has noted, "There is no mention of Baphomet either in the Templar Rule or in other medieval period Templar documents".[104] The late scholar Hugh J. Schonfield speculated that the chaplains of the Knights Templar created the term *Baphomet* through the Atbash cipher to encrypt the Gnostic term *Sophia* (Greek for "wisdom") due to the influence of hypothetical Qumran Essene

Figure 16: *Jacques de Molay, nineteenth-century color lithograph by Chevauchet*

scrolls, which they may have found during archaeological digs in the Kingdom of Jerusalem.[105]

Roman Catholic Church's position

The papal process started by Pope Clement V, to investigate both the Order as a whole and its members individually found virtually no knights guilty of heresy outside France. Fifty-four knights were executed in France by French authorities as relapsed heretics after denying their original testimonies before the papal commission; these executions were motivated by Philip's desire to prevent Templars from mounting an effective defence of the Order. It failed miserably, as many members testified against the charges of heresy in the ensuing papal investigation.Wikipedia:Citation needed

Despite the poor defense of the Order, when the papal commission ended its proceedings on June 5, 1311, it found no evidence that the Order itself held heretical doctrines, or used a "secret rule" apart from the Latin and French rules. On October 16, 1311, at the General Council of Vienne held in Dauphiné, the council voted for the maintenance of the Order.Wikipedia:Citation needed

But on March 22, 1312, Clement V promulgated the bull *Vox in excelsis* in which he stated that although there was not sufficient reason to condemn the

Order, for the common good, the hatred of the Order by Philip IV, the scandal brought about by their trial, and the likely dilapidation of the Order that would result from the trial, the Order was to be suppressed by the pope's authority over it. But the order explicitly stated that dissolution was enacted, "with a sad heart, not by definitive sentence, but by apostolic provision."

This was followed by the papal bull *Ad Providum* on May 2, 1312, which granted all of the Order's lands and wealth to the Hospitallers so that its original purpose could be met, despite Philip's wishes that the lands in France pass to him. Philip held onto some lands until 1318, and in England the crown and nobility held a great deal until 1338; in many areas of Europe the land was never given over to the Hospitaller Order, instead taken over by nobility and monarchs in an attempt to lessen the influence of the Church and its Orders. Of the knights who had not admitted to the charges, against those whom nothing had been found, or those who had admitted but been reconciled to the Church, some joined the Hospitallers (even staying in the same Templar houses); others joined Augustinian or Cistercian houses; and still others returned to secular life with pension. In Portugal and Aragon, the Holy See granted the properties to two new Orders, the Order of Christ and the Order of Montesa respectively, made up largely of Templars in those kingdoms. In the same bull, he urged those who had pleaded guilty be treated "according to the rigours of justice."Wikipedia:Citation needed

In the end, the only three accused of heresy directly by the papal commission were Jacques de Molay, Grand Master of the Knights Templar, and his two immediate subordinates; they were to renounce their heresy publicly, when de Molay regained his courage and proclaimed the order's and his innocence along with Geoffrey de Charney. The two were arrested by French authorities as relapsed heretics and burned at the stake in 1314. Their ashes were then ground up and dumped into the Seine, so as to leave no relics behind.Wikipedia:Citation needed

In England the Crown was also deeply in debt to the Templars, and probably on that basis, the Templars were also persecuted in England, their lands forfeited and taken by others, (the last private owner being the favorite of Edward II, Hugh le Despenser). Many of Templars in England were killed; some fled to Scotland and other places.[106] In France, Philip IV, who was also coincidentally in terrible financial debt to the Templars was perhaps the more aggressive persecutor. So widely was the injustice of Philip's rage against the Templars perceived that the "Curse of the Templars" became legend: Reputedly uttered by the Grand Master Jacques de Molay upon the stake whence he burned, he adjured: "Within one year, God will summon both Clement and Philip to His Judgment for these actions." The fact that both rulers died within a year, as

Figure 17: *Two Templars burned at the stake, including Jacques de Molay, from a French 15th-century manuscript*

predicted, only heightened the scandal surrounding the suppression of the Order. The source of this legend does not date from the time of the execution of Jacques de Molay.[107]

Chinon and Absolution

In September 2001, Barbara Frale discovered a copy of the Chinon Parchment dated 17–20 August 1308 in the Vatican Secret Archives, a document that indicated that Pope Clement V absolved the leaders of the Order in 1308. Frale published her findings in the *Journal of Medieval History* in 2004 In 2007, The Vatican published the Chinon Parchment as part of a limited edition of 799 copies of *Processus Contra Templarios*.[108] Another Chinon parchment dated 20 August 1308 addressed to Philip IV of France, well known to historians,[109,110,111] stated that absolution had been granted to all those Templars that had confessed to heresy "and restored them to the Sacraments and to the unity of the Church".[112,113]

References and further reading

<templatestyles src="Template:Refbegin/styles.css" />
- Malcolm Barber, *The New Knighthood: A History of the Order of the Temple*. Cambridge University Press, 1994. ISBN 0521420415
- Malcolm Barber, *The Trial of the Templars*, Second edition. New York: Cambridge University Press, 2006 (hardback, ISBN 0521856396; paperback, ISBN 0521672368)
- Alan Butler, Stephen Dafoe, *The Warriors and the Bankers: A History of the Knights Templar from 1307 to the present*, Templar Books, 1998. ISBN 0968356729
- Barbara Frale, *The Knights Templar – The secret history revealed*, Maverick House Publishers; 2009. ISBN 978-1905379606
- Michael Haag, *The Tragedy of the Templars*, Profile Books, London 2012. ISBN 978-1846684500
- Michael Haag, *The Templars: History and Myth*, Profile Books, London 2008. ISBN 978-1846681486
- Sławomir Majoch (ed.). *The Knights Templar: History & Myth*[114], District Museum: Toruń (Poland), 2004. ISBN 8387083720
- Sean Martin, *The Knights Templar: History & Myths*, 2005. ISBN 1560256451
- Helen Nicholson, *The Knights Templar: A New History*, Sutton Publishing, 2001. ISBN 0750925175
- Peter Partner, *The Knights Templar and their Myth*, Destiny Books; Reissue edition, 1990. ISBN 0892812737
- Hans Prutz (trans. Dr. E. Kiernan), *The Secret Teaching of the Knights Templar*, Aontau 2006. ISBN 978-3936730029
- Dr. Karen Ralls, *The Templars and the Grail*, Quest Books, 2003. ISBN 0835608077
- Piers Paul Read, *The Templars*, Phoenix Press, 1990. ISBN 0753810875
- George Smart, *The Knights Templar: Chronology*, Authorhouse, 2005. ISBN 1418498890
- Julien Théry, "Philip the Fair, the Trial of the 'Perfidious Templars' and the Pontificalization of the French Monarchy", in *Journal of Medieval Religious Culture*, 39/2 (2013), pp. 117-148, online[115]

- *The History Channel, Decoding the Past: The Templar Code* documentary, 2005

External links

- 1917 Catholic Encyclopedia: Knights Templar, as hosted by Newadvent.com[116]
- Templar History Magazine[117]
- The Knights Templar in Slovakia[118]
- Confession Of Sins To A Priest[119]
- The Knights Templar International[120]

Chinon Parchment

The **Chinon Parchment** is a historical document discovered in September, 2001, by Barbara Frale, an Italian paleographer at the Vatican Secret Archives. On the basis of the Parchment, she has claimed that, in 1308, Pope Clement V absolved the last Grand Master, Jacques de Molay, and the rest of the leadership of the Knights Templar from charges brought against them by the Medieval Inquisition.

The Parchment is dated August 17–20, 1308, at Chinon, France, and was written by Bérenger Fredoli, Etienne de Suisy and Landolfo Brancacci, Cardinals who were of Saints Nereus and Achileus, St. Cyriac in Thermis and Sant'Angelo in Pescheria respectively. The Vatican keeps an authentic copy with reference number Archivum Arcis Armarium D 218, the original having the number D 217 (see below for the other Chinon Parchment published by Étienne Baluze in 1693).

The existence of this document has long been assumed. In the bull Faciens misericordiam, promulgated in August 1308, Clement V explained that Templar leaders were supposed to be brought to Poitiers in order to be questioned by the Pope himself, but "since some of them were so unwell at that time that they could not ride and could not by any means be brought into our (*i.e. the Pope's*) presence" three cardinals were sent out to perform the necessary inquiries at Chinon.[121] The commissioned envoys were instructed to create an official record of their investigations and, according to the bull, upon returning they presented the Pope with "the confessions and testimonies of the aforementioned Master and Commanders written down as spoken as a legal record by notarial attestation."[122] In addition, a letter exists, supposedly written by the three cardinals to King Philip IV, in which they inform him of the absolution granted to the high-ranking officers of the Knights Templar (published by Étienne Baluze).[123] The text of the Chinon Parchment is also supported by records in register *Avignonese 48* of the Vatican Secret Archives, published in *Processus Contra Templarios*.[124]

History

In late June and early July 1308 a large group of previously arrested Knights Templar appeared before Pope Clement V and his commissioners in Poitiers. Five high-ranking members of the Order, including its Grand Master Jacques de Molay, were also supposed to be delivered to the Curia, but they were diverted to Chinon (less than 60 miles away from Poitiers). After the Knights Templar present in Poitier were questioned and confessed their sins (generally following the lines of their previous testimonies given to French inquisitors) they were granted plenary absolution by the Pope on July 2, 1308.[125] Clement V understood that his inquiry could not be complete without interrogating the leaders of the Order who remained at Chinon. The Pope arranged for three cardinals to visit Chinon as his plenipotentiaries. This allowed Clement V to finalize another stage of addressing the issue of the Knights Templar trials.

An investigation was carried out by agents of the Pope to verify claims against the accused in the castle of Chinon in the diocese of Tours. According to this document and another Chinon Parchment (see below), Pope Clement V instructed cardinals to conduct the investigation of the accused Knights Templar. The cardinals therefore

> declare through this official statement directed to all who will read it . . . [that] the very same lord Pope wishing and intending to know the pure, complete, and uncompromised truth from the leaders of the said Order, namely Brother Jacques de Molay, Grandmaster of the Order of Knights Templar, Brother Raymbaud de Caron, Preceptor [of] the commandaries of Templar Knights in Outremer, Brother Hugo de Pérraud, Preceptor of France, Brother Geoffroy de Gonneville, Preceptor of Aquitania and Poitou, and Geoffroy de Charney, Preceptor of Normandy, ordered and commissioned us specifically and by his verbally expressed will in order that we might with diligence examine the truth by questioning the grandmaster and the aforementioned preceptors one-by-one and individually, having summoned notaries public and trustworthy witnesses. (Chinon Parchment dated August 17–20, 1308)

Raymbaud de Caron was the first to be interrogated, on August 17, 1308.

> After this oath, by the authority of [the] lord Pope specifically granted to us for that purpose, we extended to this humbly asking Brother Raymbaud, in a form accepted by the Church, the mercy of pardon from the verdict of excommunication that had been incurred by the aforementioned deeds, restoring him to unity with the Church and reinstating him to the communion of the faithful and the sacraments of the Church. (Chinon Parchment dated August 17–20, 1308)

Also interrogated on August 17 were Geoffroy de Charney and, third, Geoffroy de Gonneville. On August 19, 1308, Hugo de Pérraud was the fourth Templar to be interrogated. The Grandmaster was interrogated last, on August 20, 1308.

According to the document, all interrogations of the accused, spanning August 17 to 20, 1308, were always in the presence of the notaries public and the gathered witnesses. Among the accusations were sodomy,[126] denouncing God, illicit kisses, spitting on the cross, and worshiping an idol.

The body of the text details the appearances of the accused, their swearings-in, the charges against them, and the modes of questioning to which they were subjected. In the interrogation of de Molay,

> *When he was asked whether he had confessed to these things due to a request, reward, gratitude, favor, fear, hatred or persuasion by someone else, or the use of force, or fear of impending torture, he replied that he did not. When he was asked whether he, after being apprehended, was submitted to any questioning or torture, he replied that he did not.*

The text further details the denunciations, requests by the accused for absolution, and the granting of absolution by the agents of the pope. All this was always in the presence of witnesses. Part of the pardons given to Molay thus reads:

> *After this, we concluded to extend the mercy of pardons for these acts to Brother Jacques de Molay, the Grandmaster of the said Order, who in the form and manner described above had denounced in our presence the described and any other heresy, and swore in person on the Lord's Holy Gospel, and humbly asked for the mercy of pardon [from excommunication], restoring him to unity with the Church and reinstating him to communion of the faithful and the sacraments of the Church. Chinon Parchment dated August 17–20, 1308*

Analysis of the Chinon Parchment, as well as other materials of the Templar trials, enabled Barbara Frale to theorize on some of the secret initiation practices of the Templars. While three of the accused admitted to having been asked by their receptors during their initiation to denounce the Cross and spit upon the crucifix, their stories are inconsistent. Geoffroy de Gonneville, for example, stated that he had not succumbed under duress to denouncing and spitting on the Cross; despite this, he was admitted to the order, implying that the denial of the cross may have been a test of some sort. The other accused men admitted to "denouncing in words only, not in spirit". Gordon Napier thinks that the practice of the denial of the cross was training for what the new knights might later face, were they taken prisoner by Saracens.[127]

All the accused denied practicing sodomy or ever witnessing it;[128] However, kisses were admitted, having been given as a sign of respect only during Templar initiation.

Hugo de Pérraud alone stated that, during his initiation, he had been told "to abstain from partnership with women, and, if they were unable to restrain their lust, to join themselves with brothers of the Order". And only Hugo de Pérraud claimed to see the "head of an idol" the Templars were accused of worshiping, in Montpellier, in the possession of Brother Peter Alemandin, Preceptor of Montpellier. All other Templars mentioned in the Chinon Parchment denied being encouraged to "join" with other brothers, and none of the others was asked about an idol.

All added that, as with any Roman Catholic, any transgressions of the Roman Catholic faith were fully confessed to a priest or bishop, penances made, and absolutions granted.

The Chinon Parchment itself was prepared by Robert de Condet, cleric of the diocese of Soissons and an apostolic notary; the other apostolic notaries public were Umberto Vercellani, Nicolo Nicolai de Benvenuto, and Master Amise d'Orléans le Ratif. Witnesses to the proceedings were Brother Raymond (abbot of the Benedictine monastery of St. Theofred, in the diocese of Annecy), Master Berard (or Bernard?) de Boiano (archdeacon of Troia), Raoul de Boset (confessor and canon from Paris), and Pierre de Soire (overseer of Saint-Gaugery in Cambresis). According to the surviving Parchment, the other notaries public made three other, more detailed copies. All documents were sealed and signed by the participants. According to the Parchment,

> Their words and confessions were written down exactly in the way that they are included here by the notaries whose names are listed below, in the presence of witnesses [also] listed below. We also ordered that these things be drawn up in this official form and validated by the protection of our seals. (Chinon Parchment dated August 17–20, 1308)

The Chinon Parchment details a failed attempt by the Pope to preserve the Templars from the machinations of King Philip IV of France, through establishing that the Order was not heretical and was capable of reform under the aegis of the Church. However, as it became apparent that Philip had determined upon the extermination of the Order (and the confiscation of its considerable wealth and property within his kingdom), the Pope was forced to abandon the Templars to their fates by the threat of military force from the King. Outside France, the dissolution of the Order was achieved with far less bloodshed, and surviving members of the order were absorbed into other religious institutions.

Significance

In September, 2001, Barbara Frale, MA, found a copy of the parchment in the Vatican Secret Archives. Frale published her discoveries in the *Journal of Medieval History*[129] and has written a book on the subject, *Il papato e il processo ai templari*.[130]

In 2007, The Vatican published the Chinon Parchment as part of a limited edition of 799 copies of *Processus Contra Templarios* after centuries of obscurity, with an eight-hundredth (unnumbered) copy being presented to Pope Benedict XVI.

Another Chinon Parchment

Another Chinon parchment has long been known to historians,[131,132,133] having been published by Étienne Baluze in 1693[134] and by Pierre Dupuy in 1751.[135] This other parchment is dated August 20, 1308, also at Chinon; it was written by cardinals Bérenger Fredol (cardinal priest of Saints Nereus and Achileus), Etienne de Suisy (cardinal priest of Saint Cyriac in Thermis), and Landolfo Brancaccio (deacon of Sant'Angelo in Pescheria). Addressed to Philip IV of France, the parchment states that absolution had been granted to all those Templars who had confessed to heresy, and that the writers had "restored them to the Sacraments and to the unity of the Church".

References

- Barber, Malcolm, *The Trial of the Templars* (Cambridge) 1978.
- Grishin, A. A., *The Knights Templar Absolution: The Chinon Parchment and the History of the Poor Knights of Christ*. CreateSpace, 2013
- Frale, Barbara. " The Chinon chart. Papal absolution to the last Templar, Master Jacques de Molay[136]". *Journal of Medieval History*, **30**,.2, April 2004, pp. 109–134
- Frale, Barbara. *Il papato e il processo ai templari : l'inedita assoluzione de Chinon alla luce della diplomatica pontificia*. Le edizioni del Mulino. 2004
- Frale, Barbara. *Processus contra Templarios* Vatican Secret Archive. 2007.
- Haag, Michael. *The Templars: History and Myth*, Profile Books, London 2008.
- Frale, Barbara. *The Templars: The secret history revealed*, Maverick House Publishers, Dunboyne 2009.

External links

- Vatican Secret Archives Employees: Barbara Frale, MA[137]
- Le edizioni del Mulino Foreign Rights[138]
- "The Parchment of Chinon—The Absolution of Pope Clement V of the Leading Members of the Templar Order"[139]. Vatican Library. August 17–20, 1308. Archived from the original[140] on 2007-10-11. Retrieved 2007-10-12.
- The Chinon Parchment, a rough English translation[141] - InRebus.com

Organization

List of Knights Templar

Part of a series on the	
Knights Templar	
Poor Fellow-Soldiers of Christ and of the Temple of Solomon	
Overview	
<ul><li>History</li><li>Latin Rule</li><li>Seal</li><li>Grand Masters</li><li>Members</li><li>Trials and dissolution</li></ul>	
Papal bulls	
<ul><li>*Omne datum optimum* (1139)</li><li>*Milites Templi* (1144)</li><li>*Militia Dei* (1145)</li><li>*Pastoralis praeeminentiae* (1307)</li><li>*Faciens misericordiam* (1308)</li><li>*Ad providam* (1312)</li><li>*Vox in excelso* (1312)</li></ul>	
Locations	
<ul><li>France</li><li>England</li><li>Scotland</li><li>Spain</li><li>Portugal</li></ul>	
Successors	

- ▮▮ Sovereign Military Order of Malta
- ▮ Order of Christ
- ▮ Supreme Order of Christ
- ▮ Order of Montesa

Cultural references

- Non nobis
- Baphomet
- In popular culture

See also

- Military order (monastic society)
- Category:Catholic chivalric orders

▮ **Catholicism portal**

- v
- t
- e[142]

This is a list of some **members of the Knights Templar**, a powerful Christian military order during the time of the Crusades. At peak, the Order had approximately 20,000 members.

The Knights Templar were led by the Grand Master, originally based in Jerusalem, whose deputy was the Seneschal. Next in importance was the Marshal, who was responsible for individual commanders, horses, arms and equipment. He usually carried the standard or nominated a standard-bearer. The Commander of the Kingdom of Jerusalem was the treasurer and shared some authority with the Grand Master, balancing his power. Other cities also had Commanders with specific regional responsibilities.

The Grand Master and his Seneschal ruled over eight Templar provincial Masters in Europe, who were responsible for Apulia, Aragon (Spain), England, France, Hungary, Poitiers, Portugal and Scotland.

The bulk of the fighting force was made up of knights and sergeants. Knights, who usually came from the nobility, were the most prestigious and wore the white mantle and red cross over their armour, carried knightly weapons, rode horses and had the services of a squire. Sergeants filled other roles such as blacksmith or mason as well as fighting in battle. There were also squires who performed the task of caring for the horses.

For a separate list of Grand Masters, see Grand Masters of the Knights Templar.

Early members

- Hugues de Payens (founder member, 1118) (first Grand Master, 1118–1136)
- Godfrey de Saint-Omer (founder member, 1118)
- André de Montbard (founder member, 1118) (later Grand Master, 1153–1156)
- Hugues de Champagne (1125)
- Fulk V, Count of Anjou,[143] occurs 1119, 1120 or 1121

Apulia (Now part of Italy)

Masters of Apulia

- Fr. Boniface (1167)
- Guillaume de la Fossa (1186–1188)
- Pons Rigaud (1199–1205)
- Armand de Perigors (1205–1232) (afterwards Grand Master, 1232–1244)
- Jacques de Turisellis
- Damase de Fenolar (1255)
- Etienne de Sissey (1264–1271)
- Guillaume de Beaujeu (1273) (afterwards Grand Master, 1273–1291)
- Pierre de Greffier
- Guillaume de Cannelis
- Albert de Cannelis
- Geoffroy de Pierrevert
- Pierre d'Outremont
- Laurent de Beaune (1300)
- Ode de Vaudrie (1307)

Source:

Aragon (East Spain)

Masters of Aragon

All the dates given are those of the first record as master and of the last. Rarely is the date of appointment or end of tenure known.

The following were *de facto* provincial masters before the formal creation of an Aragonese province:

- Hugh of Rigaud (1128–1136)
- Raymond Gaucebert (1134)
- Arnold of Bedocio (1136)

The following were "masters in Provence and certain parts of Spain":

- **Pere de Rovira** (*Pere de la Rovira*; November 1143 – January 1158) First Brother to hold the title of Provincial Master
- Hugh of Barcelona (1159 – April 1162)
- Hugh Geoffrey (*Hugues Godefroi*; May 1163 – 1166)
- Arnold of Torroja (*Arnaud de Toroge*; October 1166 – March 1181) (afterwards Grand Master 1181–1184)
- Berenguer of Avinyó (*Bérenger d'Avignon*; April 1181 – March 1183)
- Guy of Sellón (April–June 1183)
- Lorencio Plaza; November 1184)
- Raymond of Canet (November 1183 – July 1185)
- Gilbert Eral (*Gilbert Erail*; October 1185 – August 1189) (afterwards Grand Master 1193–1200)
- Pons (of) Rigaud (September 1189 – February 1195)
- Gerald of Caercino (February 1196)
- Arnold of Claramunt (*Arnaud de Clairmont*; April – November 1196)
- Pons Marescalci (Dec. 1196 – June 1199)
- Arnold of Claramunt (August 1199 – April 1200), second time
- Raymond of Gurb (*Raimon de Gurp*; April 1200 – Nov. 1201)
- Pons (of) Rigaud (April 1202 – July 1206), second time
- Pedro de Monteagudo (*Pierre de Montaigu*; July 1207 – June 1212) (later Grand Master, 1218–1232)
- William Cadell (October 1212 – May 1213)
- William of Montrodón (January 1214 – September 1218)
- Evelio Ramirez born October 8 death Friday, October 13, 1307 lieutenant, cousin of James 11.
  - Adémar de Claret (1216–1218), lieutenant
  - Pons Menescal (1218–1221), lieutenant
- William of Azylach (*Guillem d'Alliac*; February 1221 – July 1223)
- Riperto of Puig Guigone (January 1224)
- Fulk of Montpesat (*Fulcon de Montpezat*; 1224 – Dec. 1227)
- William Cadell (March 1229 – June 1232), second time
- Raymond Patot (*Raimon Patot*; May 1233 – April 1234)
- Hugh of Montlaur (May 1234 – April 1238)
- Stephen of Belmonte (June – November 1239)

The following were "masters in Aragon", which also included Catalonia, Roussillon, Navarre, and eventually Majorca, Valencia, and Murcia:

- Raymond of Serra (May 1240 – June 1243)
- William of Cardona (January 1244 – May 1252)
- Hugh of Jouy (September 1254 – June 1247 / March 1258)
- William of Montañana (May 1258 – February 1262)

- William of Pontóns (March 1262 – August 1266)
- Arnold of Castellnou (March 1267 – February 1278)
- Peter of Moncada (April 1279 – October 1282)
- Berenguer of San Justo (April 1283 – May 1290)
- Berenguer of Cardona (June 1291 – January 1307)
- Simon of Lenda (September 1307)

Note also Peter Peronet, commander of Burriana in 1276.

Source

- Forey, A. J. (1974). *Templars in the Corona de Aragón*[144]. Oxford: Oxford University Press.

Czech lands

The Czech lands (or the Lands of the Bohemian Crown) now form the Czech Republic.

- 1286 – Fridericus de Silvester
- 1292 – Berthramus dictus de Czweck, preceptor Niemiec, Sławii i Morawii, w 1294
- 1291 – Bernhard von Eberstein, w 1295

England

Masters of England

- Fr. William Heath (1153–1156)
- Hugues d'Argentein
- Hoston de Saint-Omer (1153–1155)
- Richard de Hastings (1155–1185)
- Geoffroy Fitzstephen (1185–1195)
- Robert de Neuham (1195–1200)
- Thomas Bérard (1200)
- Fr. Alain (1205)
- Guillaume Cadeil (1214)
- Sir Roger St. Leger (1217)
- Aimery de Sainte-Maure (1215–1219)
- Guillaume de la Gravelle (1220)
- Alain Martel (1220–1228)
- Fr. Aimery (1228)
- Robert de Montfort (1234)
- Robert de Sandford (1235–1241)
- Fr. Amblard (1250)

- Roncelin de Fos (1252–1259)
- Robert de Sandford (1259)
- Humbert de Pairaud (1270)
- Gui de Foresta (1275)
- Robert de Torteville (1276)
- Henri de Faverham (1277–1278)
- Robert de Torteville (1280)
- Gui de Foresta (1288)

+Robert de Haleghton (1290–1294 Yorkshire)

- Guillaume de Tourville (1292)
- Gui de Foresta (1293–1296)
- Brian le Jay (1296–1298)
- Guillaume de la More (1298–1307)

source: +source:[145]

Others

- Robert of St. Albans (d. 1187), converted to Islam and married Saladin's niece, according to Roger of Howden[146]
- Hugh de Paduinan
- Richard Mallebeench, Master of the Templars in England
- Gilbert of Ogerstan, caught stealing money from the Saladin tithe, 1188[147]
- Sir Lachlan MacLean-de Corzon (d.1194) Baron of ak'ham, fought in the Third Crusade
- Sir William de Harcourt, 1216, fought at Siege of Damietta.
- Sir Allen William Howard of Norfolk (d.1239), fought in the Third Crusade
- Amberaldus, Master of the Templars in England
- Richord Brand, Conqueror of Tyre
- William de Ferrers, 3rd Earl of Derby, fought in the Third Crusade
- Gilbert de Lacy, Precentor of the Templars and a commander in the 1160s
- William Marshal, 1st Earl of Pembroke, invested as a knight on his deathbed
- Elyas de Rolleston, 1270, fought in the Eighth Crusade[148]

France

Masters of France

- Marcus Adrienn LeBlanc
- Sir Geoffrey de Charney
- Sir Jean De St. Leger (1096)
- Payen de Montdidier (1130)
- Robert de Craon (died in 1147) (afterwards Grand Master 1136–1147)
- Everard des Barres (1143–1147) (afterwards Grand Master 1147–1151)
- Guillaume Pavet (1160–1161)
- Geoffroy Foucher (1171)
- David de Rancourt (1171–1175)
- Eustache le Chien (1175–1179)
- Robert de Miliaco (1190)
- Raoul de Montliard (1192–1193)
- Gilbert Erail (1196)
- Arn Fredrik LeBlanc (1203)
- André de Coulours (1204)
- Guillaume Oeil-de-Boeuf (1207)
- André de Coulours (1208–1219)
- Guillaume de l'Aigle (1222)
- Fr. Aimard (1222–1223)
- Eudes Royier (1225)
- Olivier de la Roche (1225–1228)
- Pons d'Albon (1229)
- Robert de Lille (1234)
- Pons d'Albon (1236–1240)
- Fr. Damase (lieut.) (1241–1242)
- Renaud de Vichier (1242–1249) (afterwards Grand Master 1250–1256)
- Gui de Basenville (1251–1253)
- Fabienn Deon LeBlanc (1253–1258
- Foulques de Saint-Michel (1256–1258)
- Humbert de Pairaud (1261–1264)
- Amaury de la Roche (1265–1271)
- Jean le Francois (1277–1281)
- Guillaume de Mallay (1286)
- Hugues de Pairaud (1291–1294)
- Matthew John Norris (1294–1299)
- Gérard de Villiers (1299–1307)
- Jerar de Poitous (1307)

Source:

Les commandeurs de Richerenches

1. Arnaud de Bedos (1136–1138)
2. Gérard de Montpierre (1138–1139)
3. Hugues de Bourbouton (1139–1141)
4. Hugues de Panaz (1141–1144)
5. Hugues de Bourbouton (1145–1151)
6. Déodat de l'Etang (1151–1161)
7. Guillaume de Biais (1161)
8. Déodat de l'Etang (1162–1173)
9. Foulques de Bras (1173–1179)
10. Pierre Itier (1179)
11. Hugolin (1180–1182)
12. Raimond (1200–1203)
13. Déodat de Bruissac (1205–1212)
14. Jeremy Bermond (1216–1220)
15. David Potterific (1220–1230)
16. Bertrand de la Roche (1230)
17. Roustan de Comps (1232)
18. Raymond Seguis (1244)
19. Raymond de Chambarrand (1260–1280)
20. Ripert Dupuy (1280–1288)
21. Nicholis Laseter (1288–1300)
22. Pons d'Alex (1300–1304)
23. Raimbaud Alziari (1304)
24. Guillaume Hugolin (1308)
25. Robert de Sablé Master (1191–1193)

Source:[149]

Les Commandeurs du Ruou

1. Hugues Raimond (de Villacros) 1170
2. Pons de Rigaud 1180
3. Bertrand de Gardannes 1195
4. Bertrand Hugues 1195
5. Bernard Aimeric (Vice Précepteur) 1203
6. Bernard de Claret (Précepteur) 1205
7. G. Gralons 1205
8. Bernard de Clairet de Claret 1206
9. Roger (Vice Précepteur) 1215
10. Rostang de Comps 1216
11. R. Laugier (Précepteur) 1222
12. Rostang de Comps 1224

13. R. Laugier (Précepteur) 1229
14. Pons Vitrerius 1233
15. Rostang de Comps 1235
16. Pierre de Boisesono Boysson 1236
17. Ugues de Milmeranda 1241
18. Rostang de Comps 1248
19. Rostang de Boiso ou Buxo de Buis 1251
20. Guillaume de Mujoul (Précepteur) 1255
21. Alaman 1256
22. Rostang de Boiso de Buis 1260
23. Boncarus (Précepteur) 1265
24. Albert Blacas 1269
25. Pierre Geoffroi 1284
26. Albert Blacas de Baudinard 1298
27. Hugues de Rocafolio 1305
28. Bertrand de Silva de la Selve (Précepteur) 1307
29. Geoffroy de Pierrevert 1308
30. Geoffrey de Campion 1310

Sources:[150,151]

Visitors of France and Poitou

- Geoffroy Foucher (1164)
- Gauthier de Beyrouth (1166–1168)
- Geoffroy Foucher (1168–1171)
- Eustache le Chien (1171–1173) (afterwards Master of France, 1175)
- Albert de Vaux (1173–1174)
- Baudouin de Gand (1176–1178)
- Aimé de Ayes (1179–1188)
- Eluard de Neuville (1188–1190)
- Gilbert Erail (1190–1193) (afterwards Master of France, 1196)
- Pons Rigaud (1193–1198)
- Aimé de Ayes (1202–1206)
- Pons Rigaud (1207–1208)
- Guillaume Oeil-de-Boeuf (1208–1211) (previously Master of France, 1207)
- Guillaume Cadeil (1212–1216)
- Alain Martel (1221) (also Master of England 1220–1228)
- Hugues de Montilaur (1234–1237)
- Pierre de Saint-Romain (1237–1242)
- Raimbaud de Caromb (1246)
- Renaud de Vichier (1246–1250)

- Hugues de Jouy (1251)
- Constant de Hoverio
- Gui de Basenville (1257–1262)
- Humbert de Pairaud (1266–1269) (afterwards Master of England, 1270)
- Francon de Bort(1270–1273)
- Hugues Raoul (1273)
- Pons de Brozet (1274–1280)
- Geoffroy de Vichier (1286–1290)
- Hugues de Pairaud (1291–1307) (also Master of France, 1291–1294)

Source:

Germany

- Gebhard Preceptori domorum milicie Templi per Alemanniam 1241, 1244Wikipedia:Citation needed
- Johannes Magistro summo preceptore milicie Templi per Teutoniam, per Boemiam, per Morauiam et per Poloniam 1251
- Widekind Domum militi Templi in Alemania et Slauia preceptor Magister domorum militie Templi per Alemaniam et Poloniam 1261, 1268, 1271, 1279
- R de Grae'ubius Preceptor domorum milicie Templi per Alemanniam et Slavia 1280 ?–1284
- Friedrich Wildegraf Preceptor domorum milicie Templi per Alemanniam et Slauiam 1288–1292
- Bertram gen. Czwek (von Esbeke) Commendator fratrum domus militie Templi in Almania, Bohemia, Polonia et Moravia 1294–1297
- Friedrich von Alvensleben Domorum milicie Templi per Alemaniam et Slauiam preceptor 1303–1308
- Hugo de Grumbach Grand master of Germany 1310 ?
- Otto von Brunswick, Comtur of the Order of Knights Templar at Süpplingenburg 1303–1304
- Lord Johan Kraus 1304–1307
- Ruprecht Dilber 1194
    - **Lieutenants**
    - Jordanus von Esbeke domus milicie Templi per Alemaniam et Slauiam vicepreceptor 30 June 1288
    - Johan Decher (Decker) 1152–1153

Rhine

- Alban von Randecke Rhine 1306
- Friedrich Wildegraf Rhine 1308

Hungary and Croatia

Leaders of Knights Templar in Hungary had official title "masters of Knights Templar for Hungary and Slavonia" (meaning Croatia) (*maestro della militia del tempio per Ungariam et Sclavoniam*).[152]

Masters of Hungary and Croatia

- Fr. Cuno
- Fr. Gauthier
- Fr. Jean
- Pons de la Croix (1215)
- Johannes Gottfried von Schluck (1230)
- Rembald de Voczon (1241)
- Thierry de Nuss (1247)
- Raimbaud de Caromb
- Jacques de Montreal
- Fr. Widekind (1271–1279)
- Gérard de Villers
- Frédéric wildgrave de Salm (1289)
- Bertram von Esbeke (1296)
- Frédéric de Nigrip
- Frédéric von Alvensleben (1300)

Source:

Slavonia

- brother Dominic (biological brother of Ban Borić)[153]

Poitiers (Now part of France)

Masters of Poitiers

- Fr. Falco (1141)
- Guillaume Guidaugier (1141)
- Fr. Hugues (1151)
- P. Levesque (1166)
- Guillaume Pavet (1166–1173)
- Humbert Boutiers (1180)
- Aimery de Sainte-Maury (1189–1190) (later Master of England, 1215)
- Guillaume Arnauld (1201)
- Téméric Boez (1205)
- Guillaume Oeil-de-Boeuf (1207) (also Master of France, 1207)
- Giraud Brochard (1210–1222)
- Gui de Tulle (1222)
- Giraud de Broges (1223–1234)
- Guillaume de Sonnay (1236–1245)
- Foulques de Saint-Michel (1247–1253)
- Hugues Grisard (1254–1258)
- Francon de Bort (1261)
- Gui de Basenville (1262–1264)
- Humbert de Pairaud (1266–1269)
- Jean le Francois (1269–1276)
- Amblard de Vienne (1278–1288)
- Raymond de Mareuil (lieut.) (1285–1288)
- Pierre de Madic (1288–1290)
- Pierre de Villiers ou Villard (1292–1300)
- Geoffroy de Gonneville (1300–1307)

Source:

Palestine

- Guillaume 1130
- André de Montbard 1148, 1151, 1152, 1154
- Guillaume de Guirehia 1163
- Gautier 1170
- Béranger 1174, 1176
- Seiher de Mamedunc, 1174
- Godechaux de Turout, 1174
- Walter du Mesnil, 1174
- Gérard de Ridefort 1183

- Hurson 1187
- Aimon de Ais 1190
- Reric de Cortina 1191 April–July
- Bryony Bonds 1192
- F. Relis : last to hold the title of seneschal

Grand-Commanders

- Odon 1156Wikipedia:Citation needed
- Gilbert Erail 1183 (afterwards Grand Master 1193–1200)
- Jean de Terric 1188
- Gerbert 1190
- William Payne 1194
- Irmengaud 1198
- Barthélemy de Moret 1240
- Pierre de Saint-Romain 1241
- Gilles 1250 (February)
- Étienne d'Outricourt 1250 (May)
- Amaury de la Roche 1262 (May)
- Guillaume de Montignane 1262 (December)
- Simon de la Tour ????
- G. de Salvaing 1273
- Arnaud de Châteauneuf 1277–1280
- Thibaud Gaudin (afterwards Grand Master 1291–1292)

Marshals

- Hugues de Quilioco 1154Wikipedia:Citation needed
- Robert Franiel 1186
- Jacques de Maillé 1187
- Geoffroy Morin 1188
- Adam 1198
- Guillaume d'Arguillières 1201
- Hugues de Montlaur 1244
- Renaud Vichier 1250
- Hugues de Jouy 1252
- Étienne de saisi 1260
- Guillaume de Molay 1262
- Gimblard 1270
- Guy de Foresta (Forest) 1277–1288?
- Pierre de Severy 1291
- Sir Jarim de'Varean 1295
- Barthélémy 1302
- Aimon(Aimé) d'Osiliers 1316[154]

Poland

- 1134–? – Geoffroy from Płock
- 1139–1148 – Bernhardt
- ?–1155 – Joseph
- 1189–? – Thibault from Halych
- ?–1190 – Mieszko
- ?–? – Jan
- ?–1194 – Guillem Ramond
- ?–1198 – Janusz from Kijów
- 1200–1208 – Jan from Potok
- 1201–1223 – Mieszko from Lwów
- 1229–1251 – Lukasz
- 1229–1241 – Mieszko from Lwów
- ?–? – Zbyszko from Kraków
- ?–? – Andrzej from Toruń
- ?–? – Jurand from Płock
- 1251–1256 – Janusz
- 1258–1259 – Ratka from Wilno
- 1261–1263 – Fridericus
- 1273–1281 – Mieszko from Wilno
- 1284–1290 – Lukasz
- 1285–1291 – Bernhard von Eberstein Humilis preceptor domorum milicie Templi per Poloniam, Sclauiam, Novam TerramPreceptori et fratribus militie Templi in partibus Polonie, Pomeranie, Cassubie, Cracouie et Slauie 13 November 1291 – 1295
- 1294 – Sanderus
- 1296–1303 – Jordanus von Esbeke / preceptor /
- 1301–1312 – Jan from Halych
- 1303 – brat Fryderyk von Alvensleben
- 1305 – Dietrich von Lorenen
- 1309–1312 – Janusz from Halych

Source:[155]

Portugal

Masters of Portugal

- Arnaldo da Rocha? (In the 16th, 17th and 18th centuries, some authors and chroniclers of the history of the Portuguese Templar Order and its continuer, the Order of Christ, possibly based on original medieval source material in Braga and Tomar, cite the Portuguese Pedro Arnaldo da Rocha, of Borgundian and French parentage, as having been one of the founding knights of the militia of the Poor Knights of Christ and of the Temple of Solomon in Jerusalem, alongside Gondemare, and then in Portugal)[156]
- Gondamer or Gondemare? (the same authors identify one of the 9 founders of the Knights Templar, the Knight Gondemare, as having Portuguese origin – possibly from medieval Gundemar; also spelled Gundemari or Gondemare, present-day Gondomar, in the County of Portugal))[157]
- King Afonso I of Portugal, *Templar Brother* (13.03.1129); First King of Portugal (1139–1185)
- Raymond Bernard, known as Raimundo Bernardo in Portugal (1126–1135) Also possibly a provincial master

The following were masters in Portugal:

- Guilherme Ricardo 1124 (1127–1139)
- Hugo Martins (1139)
- Pedro Froilaz? (1139?–1143)
- Hugues de Montoire (1143)
- Pedro Arnaldo (1155–1158)
- Gualdim Pais 1160 (1158–1195)
- Lopo Fernandes
- Fernando Dias (1202)

The following were masters in the Province of Leon, Castile and Portugal (based in Tomar, also temporarily in Castelo Branco), or the *three kingdoms of Spain*:

- Gomes Ramires (1210–1212)
- Pedro Álvares de Alvito (1212–1221)
- Pedro Anes (1223–1224)
- Martim Sanches (1224–1229)
- Estêvão Belmonte (1229–1237)
- Guilherme Fulco alias Fouque (1237–1242)
- Martim Martins (1242–1248)
- Pedro Gomes (1248–1251)

- Paio Gomes (1251–1253)
- Martim Nunes (1253–1265)
- Gonçalo Martins (1268–1271)
- Beltrão de Valverde (1273–1277)
- João Escritor (1280–1283)
- João Fernandes (1283–1288)

The following were masters in Portugal:

- Afonso Pais-Gomes (1289–1290)
- Lourenço Martins (1291–1295)
- Vasco Fernandes (1295–1306)Wikipedia:Citation needed

Source:

Prats-de-Mollo

Family dez Coll:

- Berenger de Coll (last known survivor of Mas Deu – 1350)
- Guillem de Cardona (1247–1251)
- Hugues de Jouy (1251)
- S. de Belmonte (1269)
- Pere de Montcada (1276–1282)
- Bérenger de Cardona (1304)
- Rodrigue Ibañez (1307)

Grand Masters of the Knights Templar

Part of a series on the
Knights Templar
Poor Fellow-Soldiers of Christ and of the Temple of Solomon
Overview
<ul><li>History</li><li>Latin Rule</li><li>Seal</li><li>Grand Masters</li><li>Members</li><li>Trials and dissolution</li></ul>
Papal bulls
<ul><li>*Omne datum optimum* (1139)</li><li>*Milites Templi* (1144)</li><li>*Militia Dei* (1145)</li><li>*Pastoralis praeeminentiae* (1307)</li><li>*Faciens misericordiam* (1308)</li><li>*Ad providam* (1312)</li><li>*Vox in excelso* (1312)</li></ul>
Locations
<ul><li>France</li><li>England</li><li>Scotland</li><li>Spain</li><li>Portugal</li></ul>
Successors
<ul><li>Sovereign Military Order of Malta</li><li>Order of Christ</li><li>Supreme Order of Christ</li><li>Order of Montesa</li></ul>
Cultural references
<ul><li>Non nobis</li><li>Baphomet</li><li>In popular culture</li></ul>
See also
<ul><li>Military order (monastic society)</li><li>Category:Catholic chivalric orders</li></ul>
Catholicism portal

- v
- t
- e[158]

Part of a series on the
Hierarchy of the Catholic Church

Saint Peter

Ecclesiastical titles (order of precedence)

- Pope
- Cardinal
  - Cardinal Vicar
- Moderator of the curia
- Chaplain of His Holiness
- Papal legate
- Papal majordomo
- Apostolic Nuncio
- Apostolic Delegate
- Apostolic Syndic
- Apostolic visitor
- Vicar Apostolic
- Apostolic Exarch
- Apostolic Prefect
- Assistant at the Pontifical Throne
- Eparch
- Metropolitan
- Patriarch
- Bishop
  - Archbishop
  - Bishop Emeritus
  - Diocesan bishop
  - Major archbishop
  - Primate
  - Suffragan bishop
  - Titular bishop
  - Coadjutor bishop
  - Auxiliary bishop
- Territorial prelate

- Territorial abbot

- Catholicism portal
- v
- t
- e[159]

Each man who held the position of Grand Master of the Knights Templar was the supreme commander of the *Poor Fellow-Soldiers of Christ and of the Temple of Solomon* (also known as the **Knights Templar**), starting with founder Hugues de Payens in 1118. While many Grand Masters chose to hold the position for life, abdication was not unknown. Some masters chose to leave for life in monasteries or diplomacy. Grand Masters often led their knights into battle on the front line and the numerous occupational hazards of battle made some tenures very short.

Each country had its own Master, and the Masters reported to the Grand Master. He oversaw all of the operations of the Order, including both the military operations in the Holy Land and eastern Europe, and the financial and business dealings in the Order's infrastructure of western Europe. The Grand Master controlled the actions of the order but he was expected to act the same way as the rest of the knights. After the Pope issued a Papal Bull on behalf of the Templars, the Grand Master was obliged to answer only to Rome.

List of Grand Masters

#	Arms	Name	Time in office
1.		Hugues de Payens	1118–1136
2.		Robert de Craon	1136–1147
3.		Everard des Barres	1147–1151
4.		Bernard de Tremelay †	1151–1153

5.		André de Montbard	1153–1156
6.		Bertrand de Blanchefort	1156–1169
7.		Philip of Nablus	1169–1171
8.		Odo de St Amand (POW)	1171–1179
9.		Arnold of Torroja	1181–1184
10.		Gerard de Ridefort †	1185–1189
11.		Robert de Sablé	1191–1193
12.		Gilbert Erail	1193–1200
13.		Phillipe de Plessis	1201–1208
14.		Guillaume de Chartres	1209–1219
15.		Pedro de Montaigu	1218–1232
16.		Armand de Périgord (POW)	1232–1244
17.		Richard de Bures (*Disputed*)	1244/5–1247[160]
18.		Guillaume de Sonnac †	1247–1250
19.		Renaud de Vichiers	1250–1256
20.		Thomas Bérard	1256–1273
21.		Guillaume de Beaujeu †	1273–1291
22.		Thibaud Gaudin	1291–1292

23.		Jacques de Molay	1292–1314

Figure 18: *Hugues de Payens, First Grand Master*

Figure 19: *Jacques de Molay, Last (23rd) Grand Master*

Legacy

List of Knights Templar sites

Part of a series on the
Knights Templar
Poor Fellow-Soldiers of Christ and of the Temple of Solomon
Overview
<ul><li>History</li><li>Latin Rule</li><li>Seal</li><li>Grand Masters</li><li>Members</li><li>Trials and dissolution</li></ul>
Papal bulls
<ul><li>*Omne datum optimum* (1139)</li><li>*Milites Templi* (1144)</li><li>*Militia Dei* (1145)</li><li>*Pastoralis praeeminentiae* (1307)</li><li>*Faciens misericordiam* (1308)</li><li>*Ad providam* (1312)</li><li>*Vox in excelso* (1312)</li></ul>
Locations
<ul><li>France</li><li>England</li><li>Scotland</li><li>Spain</li><li>Portugal</li></ul>
Successors

• ▓ Sovereign Military Order of Malta • ▓ Order of Christ • ▓ Supreme Order of Christ • ▓ Order of Montesa
Cultural references
• Non nobis • Baphomet • In popular culture
See also
• Military order (monastic society) • Category:Catholic chivalric orders
▓ Catholicism portal
• v • t • e[161]

With their military mission and extensive financial resources, the **Knights Templar** funded a large number of building projects around Europe and the Holy Land, many structures remain standing today.

Middle East

- The Templar Tunnel in Acre, Israel
- Château Pèlerin, Israel
- Ruad, Syria
- Chastel Blanc, Syria
- The port city and fortress of Tortosa, Syria

Cyprus

- The Twin Church of the Templars and Hospitallers, Famagusta
- Kolossi Castle

France

- Commandry of Coulommiers, France
- Commandry of Avalleur, in Bar-sur-Seine
- Commandry of Saint-Blaise, Hyères[162]
- La Rochelle, Charente Maritime, France
- Chapelle des Templiers de Metz - 12th-century Gothic chapel with octagonal plan and various paintings.
- Commandry of Libdeau, Toul - 12th-century Gothic chapel with rectangular plan and traces of paintings.[163]

List of Knights Templar sites

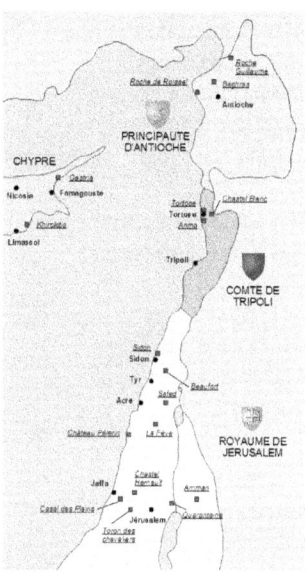

Figure 20: *Templar fortresses in the Outremer*

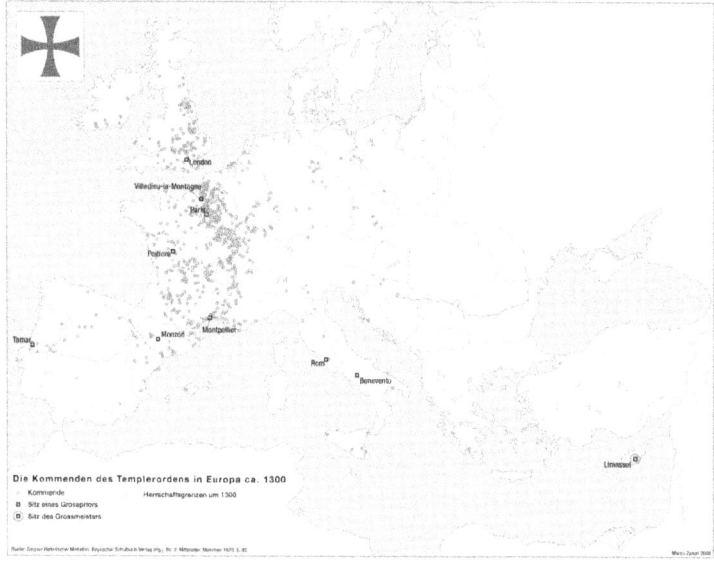

Figure 21: *Templar establishments in Europe.*

- Commandry of Sergeac
- Commandry of Dognon, Blanzac-Porcheresse - 12th-century chapel with rectangular plan and various paintings.
- Commandry of Sainte-Eulalie-de-Cernon
- Commandry of Richerenches
- La Couvertoirade, Aveyron - A castle[164], commandry and fortifications
- Commandry of Celles
- Commandry of Arville, now restored with a museum of Templar history.
- Templar fortress of Paris, now destroyed.

Portugal

- Castle of Almourol
- Castle of Idanha
- Castle of Monsanto
- Castle of Pombal
- Castle of Soure - received and reconstructed in March 1128, was the first castle of the Knights Templar.
- Old town of Tomar, including the Castle, the Convent of the Order of Christ and the Church of Santa Maria do Olival

Spain

Crown of Castilla-La Mancha

- Castle of Montalbán in San Martín de Montalbán, province of Toledo
- Castle of Villalba in Cebolla, Province of Toledo
- Castle of San Servando, in Toledo
- The Templar House, Toledo

Crown of Castile and León

- Iglesia Veracruz in Segovia
- Castillo de los Templarios in Ponferrada
- Castle of Alcañices, in Zamora

Crown of Aragon

- Peniscola Castle
- Castle of Castellote
- Castle of Miravet
- Castle of Barbens
- Castle of Gardeny, in Lérida
- Castle of Xivert in Valencia

United Kingdom
England

 Wikimedia Commons has media related to *Knights Templar*.

Sorted by county

- Temple Church, Bristol, Bristol
- Denny Abbey, Cambridgeshire
- Temple Church, Temple, Bodmin Moor, Cornwall
- St Michael's Mount, Cornwall
- Temple Sowerby, Cumbria
- Cressing Temple, Essex
- Little Maplestead, Essex
- Garway Church, Herefordshire
- Church of St Mary the Virgin in Baldock, Hertfordshire
- Temple Dinsley, Hertfordshire
- The Manor of Temple Ewell, Kent
- Rothley Temple *(Rothley Preceptory)*, Rothley, Leicestershire
- Eagle Hall Lincolnshire
- South Witham Lincolnshire
- Temple Bruer, Lincolnshire
- The Temple including Temple Church, London
  - Inner Temple
  - Middle Temple
  - Temple tube station
- Temple Mills, Stratford, London
- Temple Cowton, North Yorkshire
- Westerdale Preceptory, North Yorkshire
- Temple Cowley, Oxfordshire
- Templars Square, Oxfordshire
- Cameley and Temple Cloud, Somerset
- Templecombe, Somerset
- Keele, Staffordshire[165]
- Temple Farm, Rockley, Wiltshire
- Temple Balsall, Warwickshire
- Shipley Church, Shipley, West Sussex
- Temple Newsam, West Yorkshire
- St Mary The Virgin church, Welsh Newton, Herefordshire[166]

Scotland

- Temple, Midlothian

Ireland

- Templetown, County Wexford
- Clontarf Castle (Templar Preceptory), County Dublin
- Baldungan Church (in-ruins), Skerries, County Dublin
- Temple House, Ballymote, County Sligo[167]

Croatia

- Brckovljani,
- Fortress of Klis,
- Glogovnica
- Gora, Croatia
- Gornji Slatinik
- Hrvatska Dubica,
- Lovčić
- Našice,
- Nova Ves,
- Rassecha – Nova Rača
- Senj,
- Zdelja village near Virje
- Vižinada
- Vrana Fortress,

Italy

- San Bevignate, Perugia
- Castello della Magione, Poggibonsi
- San Pietro alla Magione, Siena
- Valvisciolo Abbey, Sermoneta
- Abbey of St. Michael in Montescaglioso

Other countries

- Tempelhof, Berlin, Germany
- Templstejn, Czech Republic
- Chwarszczany village, Poland

References

29. http://www.kuria.gliwice.pl/index.php?option=com_content&view=article&id=173:parafia-sw-bartlomieja-gliwice&catid=97&Itemid=726

Celtic Cross Templar Knights Priory of Ireland (Charter # 004)

Under the Organizational Command of the Order Knights Commander - Baron, Terence Barry Order formed October 24th 2015
http://www.celticcrossministry.com/celtic_cross_templar_knights.html
http://www.celticcrossministry.com/cctk_priory_of_ireland.html

International Organisation of Good Templars

The **International Organisation of Good Templars**, founded as the **Independent Order of Good Templars** (**IOGT**), is a fraternal organization describing itself as "the premier global interlocutor for evidence-based policy measures and community-based interventions to prevent and reduce harm caused by alcohol and other drugs". It claims to be the largest worldwide community of non-governmental organisations with a mission to independently enlighten people around the world on a lifestyle free from alcohol and other drugs. The International Organisation of Good Templars is a leading NGO in the temperance movement.

IOGT International works to promote the avoidance of alcohol and other drugs by supporting communities and societies around the world. Founded in 1851, their constitution states that this will lead to the liberation of peoples of the world, this leading to a richer, freer and more rewarding life. Today the headquarters of IOGT International are situated in Stockholm, Sweden.

History

The IOGT originated as one of a number of fraternal organizations for temperance or total abstinence founded in the 19th century and with a structure modeled on Freemasonry, using similar ritual and regalia. Unlike many, however, it admitted men and women equally, and also made no distinction by race.

In 1850, in Utica, New York, Daniel Cady founded one such organization, the Knights of Jericho. In 1851, a lodge of it in Oriskany Falls (then known as Castor Hollow), a village near Utica, was visited by 13 members of another Utica group. Under the leadership of Wesley Bailey, it was decided that these

Figure 22: *IOGT membership certificate, Michigan, 1868*[168]

two lodges form the Order of Good Templars. The motto of the renamed organization was "Friendship, Hope and Charity".

Over the next year, 14 additional lodges were established. By the summer of 1852, a convention was called in Utica to establish a Grand Lodge. During this, a dispute broke out between Wesley Bailey and Leverett Coon, who had established a lodge, Excelsior, in Syracuse. Coon left the meeting and his lodge supported his actions by seceding as the Independent Order of Good Templars, with the motto altered to "Faith, Hope and Charity". They shortly merged back, the resulting group continuing under the name Independent Order of Good Templars.

The Order first grew rapidly in the United States and in Canada. In 1868, Joseph Malins returned to his native England and established a Birmingham lodge, from which IOGT spread to Europe and the rest of the world. Within three years the Order spread to Ireland, Wales, Australia, Malta, New Zealand, France, Portugal, South Africa, Bermuda, Belgium and East India. By 1876, it had established itself in Ceylon (Sri Lanka), Madras, British Honduras, British Guyana, Jamaica, Malacca, China, Japan, Sierra Leone, St. Helena, Argentina, Trinidad, Grenada and the Bahamas. This was followed by lodges in Norway, Sweden, Denmark, Iceland, Switzerland, Germany and Jerusalem.

Figure 23: *Small assembly building of the IOGT lodge in Vågå, Norway. Built 1908.*

From 1900 and onwards, further groups were set up in the Netherlands, Burma, Nigeria and Panama.[169] In 1906, reflecting the International reach of the organisation the word "Independent" in its title, was replaced by "International".

In an attempt to modernize its image the IOGT changes some of its titles and ritualistic features in the 1970s. Use of regalia and rituals began to diminish or were eliminated. In 2003, instead of "Order", the group became the International *Organisation* of Good Templars . The title of "Chief Templar" was changed to "President" and local units were given the option of calling themselves "Chapters" rather than "Lodges". Instead of three degrees, only one, the Justice degree, was worked by 1979, and the ritual is no longer secret.[170]

Membership

In 1875, after the American Civil War, the American senior body voted to allow separate lodges and Grand Lodges for white and black members, to accommodate the practice of segregation in southern US states. In 1876, Malins and other British members failed in achieving an amendment to stop this, and left to establish a separate international body. In 1887 this and the American body were reconciled into a single IOGT.

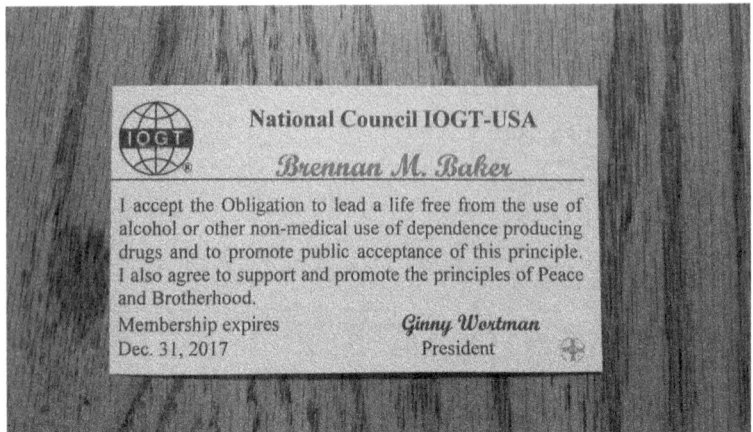

Figure 24: *Membership card for the IOGT-USA*

Women were admitted as regular members early in the history of the Good Templar. In 1979, there were 700,000 members internationally, though only 2,000 in the country of the IOGTs origin, the United States.[171]

In Europe, it has a youth division, ACTIVE.

Member organisations

As listed on the website of IOGT International[172].

- Belgium - IOGT Belgium
- Bosnia-Herzegovina - LINK
- Bulgaria - Free Youth Bulgaria
- Burundi - IOGT Burundi
- Croatia - Klub Lijecenih Alkoholikar Opcine, Klub Mladih Juvente
- Czech Republic - IOGT Czech Republic
- Denmark - IOGT Denmark
- Estonia - Juvente Estonia, IOGT Estonia, Estonian Temperance Union
- Faroe Islands - IOGT Faroe Islands
- Finland - IOGT Finland, FSNU-MHF, Raittiuden Ystävät ry., Sinuli Finland
- Gambia - IOGT Gambia
- Germany - IOGT Germany, Juvente Germany, FORUT Germany
- Ghana - IOGT Ghana
- Guinea-Bissau - IOGT Guinea-Bissau

International Organisation of Good Templars 77

- Iceland - IOGT Iceland, IOGT Junior in Island, Icelandic Temperance Youth
- India - ADIC India, Amardeep, Madras Social Service Guild, Brain Society, Temperance Association of Orissa
- Italy - GGPF Italy
- Kenya - IOGT Kenya
- Latvia - JAF Latvia, IOGT Latvia
- Lithuania - Lithuanian Temperance Society, Lithuanian Temperance Youth Federation
- Netherlands - ANDO
- Norway - IOGT Norway, Juvente Norway, IOGT Junior Organisation, DNT, FORUT Norway
- Poland - IOGT Polska[173]
- Portugal - Sociedade Anti-Alcoólica Portuguesa
- Russia - The NAN Foundation, Youth Antidrug Federation
- Senegal - IOGT Senegal, ASPAT
- Sierra Leone - IOGT Sierra Leone
- Slovakia - IOGT – Healthy Lifestyle Society, NOM
- South Africa - IOTT South
- Sri Lanka - ADIC Sri Lanka, Temperance Youth Organisation of Sri Lanka, Temperance Youth Club of Sri Lanka, All Ceylon Young Men's Muslim Association Conference, Non-Violent Direct Action Group, Sri Lanka Temperance Association, Lanka Jatilka Sarvodaya Shramadana Movement
- Sweden - IOGT-NTO, Ungdomens Nykterhetsförbund, JUNIS, Nykterhetsrörelsens Scoutförbund
- Switzerland - IOGT Switzerland, Juvente Switzerland, KiM Switzerland
- Tanzania - SOBER Tanzania
- Thailand - IOGT Thailand
- Turks & Caicos Islands - Success Lodge No.1 I.O.G.T.
- Uganda - SOBER Uganda
- Ukraine - Youth Temperance Movement "Better", Ukrainian Society for Temperance & Health
- United Kingdom - IOGT England and Wales, IOGT Scotland, National Youth Council of IOGT England
- United States - IOGT-USA
- Vietnam - IOGT Vietnam

- Others - PCDP-Cambodia, Together against Drugs, Sri Lanka Interactive Media Group, International Academy of Sobriety, EGTYF Macedonia, Atmosphere F, NADA India Foundation,

Further reading

- David M. Fahey, "How the Good Templars Began: Fraternal Temperance in New York State", Social History of Alcohol Review, Nos. 38-39 (1999)
- David M. Fahey, "Temperance & Racism: John Bull, Johnny Reb, and the Good Templars" (University Press of Kentucky, 1996).

External links

 Wikimedia Commons has media related to *International Organisation of Good Templars*.

- Official IOGT website[174]

Knights Templar (Freemasonry)

This page is about the Masonic group, for the medieval Knights, see Knights Templar and Knights Hospitaller.

Knights Templar

The United Religious, Military and Masonic Orders of the Temple and of St John of Jerusalem, Palestine, Rhodes and Malta of England and Wales and Its Provinces Overseas

	The logo of the Great Priory of England and Wales and its Provinces Overseas.
Formation	1791 (as Grand Conclave) 1895 (as Grand Priory)
Founder	Thomas Dunckerley
Type	Freemasonry
Headquarters	Mark Masons' Hall, 86 St James's Street St James's London SW1A 1PL
Location	• England and Wales
Grand Master	Paul Raymond Clement (2017-present)
Parent organization	Order of Mark Master Masons United Grand Lodge of England
Affiliations	• Grand Encampment of Knights Templar of the United States • Sovereign Great Priory of the Knights Templar of Canada • Order of the Temple - Great Priory of Scotland • Order of the Temple - Great Priory of Ireland
Website	glmm.com/kt[175]

The **United Religious, Military and Masonic Orders of the Temple and of St John of Jerusalem, Palestine, Rhodes and Malta of England and Wales and Its Provinces Overseas**, better known as the **Knights Templar**, is a Masonic body founded in its current form in 1895 which bases its esoteric symbolism on the historic Crusading orders, the Knights Templar and Knights Hospitaller (which still exists as the Knights of Malta). This order accepts freemasons "in good standing", who have been through the degrees of the Holy Royal Arch. In England, the order is headquartered at Mark Masons' Hall, London and is governed under the auspices of the Order of Mark Master Masons. The organisation has no direct lineal connection to the historical Catholic military orders from which it is named.

Although Crusader themes in Freemasonry were earlier initiated by the Jacobite, Andrew Michael Ramsay and continue to have some legacy in Scottish

Rite freemasonry, the specific "Knights Templar" fraternal order connected to Freemasonry originated from Thomas Dunckerley toward the end of the 18th century, as moves to reconcile the more rationalist Premier Grand Lodge of England with the more esoteric Antient Grand Lodge of England were underway. Men such as Dunckerley wanted to promote a concept of chivalry and Christianity within a masonic framework and founded the "Grand Conclave" in England in 1791. Subsequently, this fraternal network spread elsewhere in the Anglosphere and in the United States, the "Grand Encampment of Knights Templar", initially under DeWitt Clinton emerged in 1816. To this day, the Grand Encampment remains part of the American York Rite system.

Unlike the initial degrees conferred in a regular Masonic Lodge, which only require a belief in a Supreme Being regardless of religious affiliation, the Knights Templar is one of several additional Masonic Orders in which membership is open only to Freemasons who profess a belief in Christianity. One of the obligations entrants to the order are required to declare is to protect and defend the Christian faith. The word "United" in its full title indicates that more than one historical tradition and more than one actual order are jointly controlled within this system. The individual orders 'united' within this system are principally the Knights of the Temple (Knights Templar), the Knights of Malta, the Knights of St Paul, and only within the York Rite, the Knights of the Red Cross.

History

Knightly symbolism in Freemasonry

The earliest documented link between Freemasonry and the Crusades is the 1737 oration of the Chevalier Ramsay. This claimed that European Freemasonry came about from an interaction between crusader masons and the Knights Hospitaller.[176] This is repeated in the earliest known "Moderns" ritual, the Berne manuscript, written in French between 1740 and 1744.[177]

In 1751 Baron Karl Gotthelf von Hund und Altengrotkau began the Order of Strict Observance, which ritual he claimed to have received from the reconstituted Templar Order in 1743 in Paris. He also claimed to have met two of the "unknown superiors" who directed all of masonry, one of whom was Prince Charles Edward Stuart. The order went into decline when he failed to produce any evidence to support his claims, and was wound up shortly after his death.[178,179]

In 1779 the High Knights Templar of Ireland Lodge, Kilwinning, obtained a charter from Lodge Mother Kilwinning in Scotland. This lodge now began to grant dispensations to other lodges to confer the Knights Templar Degree.

Figure 25: *Thomas Dunckerley, founder of the Grand Conclave of England. He initiated modern Templar freemasonry.*

Some time around 1790 the Early Grand Encampment of Ireland was formed, which began to warrant Templar Lodges, and evolved into the Supreme Grand Encampment in 1836.[180] The Early Grand Encampment chartered several Scottish "encampments" one of which, having been chartered in 1805 as the "Edinburgh Encampment No. 31", then became the "Grand Assembly of Knights Templar in Edinburgh". who then sought a charter from the Duke of Kent, Grand Master of the Order in England.[181] It seems that the Templar degree had filtered into the lodges of the Antients from Ireland about 1780, and was recorded at York about the same time.[182] In the five degree system developed by the York Masons, the Knights Templar degree sat between the Master Mason and the Sublime Degree of Royal Arch.[183]

Grand Conclave of England

Templar masonry in England entered a new era in 1791, with the formation of its first Grand Conclave, with Thomas Dunckerley as Grand Master. At that time, there were eight known Templar encampments in England, the most senior being the Encampment of Redemption at York, and the Baldwyn encampment at Bristol, at whose request Dunckerley began his mission. Under his leadership, the number of encampments steadily grew until his death in 1795. Stasis then followed, until in 1805 their Royal Patron, Duke of Kent,

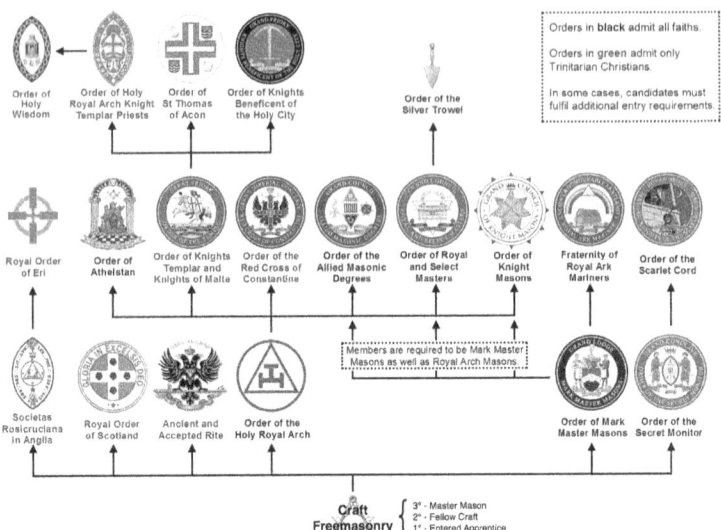

Figure 26: *The position of the United Masonic Orders of the Temple and of Malta among the appendant bodies in England and Wales*

became Grand Master himself, re-energising the society and launching it into an era of growth and development. Dunckerley laid the foundation for this not only by promoting the order, but by standardising the ritual and insisting on proper record keeping.[184] The Grand Conclave went into a period of decline between 1872 and 1895, when it was re-founded as the present day Great Priory of England and Wales.

Administration

Depending upon the geographical jurisdiction, the Knights Templar exist either as part of the York Rite or as an independent organization. Though the York Rite and the independent versions share many similarities there are key differences which are described below.

Outside the York Rite, membership is by invitation only. Candidates are required to be Master Masons, and Royal Arch Masons, and to sign a declaration that they profess the Doctrine of the Holy and Undivided Trinity. In some Australian States, the requirement of being a Royal Arch Mason no longer applies.

Local bodies of Knights Templar are known as Preceptories; local bodies of Knights of St Paul are known as Chapters; local bodies of Knights of Malta are

Figure 27: *The Cross pattée, symbol of the Order of the Temple in the independent body.*

known as Priories; all operate under a Grand or Great Priory, often with an intermediate level of Provincial Priories. Although some jurisdictions maintain a separate Great Priory of the Temple and Great Priory of Malta (as, for example, in England), the Grand Master and other officers of both Great Priories hold simultaneous equal office in both bodies. Three degrees are administered in this system:

- *The Degree of Knight Templar (Order of the Temple)*
- *The Degree of Knight of St. Paul (incorporating the Mediterranean Pass)*
- *The Degree of Knight of Malta (Order of Malta)*

In England and Wales, the "Great Priory of England and Wales" for the Masonic Knights Templar is administrated from Mark Masons' Hall, London.

The Degrees or Orders

The Illustrious Order of the Red Cross (Order of the Red Cross)

Teachings

The Order of the Red Cross continues or reverts to the period of the Royal Arch Degree when the Israelites were returning from Babylon to Jerusalem

Figure 28: *Two downward pointing swords in saltire, symbol of the Order of St Paul.*

to rebuild the Temple. Zerubbabel, their leader prevails upon King Darius to restore the Holy Vessels to the new Temple. They had been carried away by the Babylonian armies when the first Temple was destroyed. In presenting his plea before the King, the companion gives a powerful testimony to the almighty force of Truth.

The ritual places the candidate in the role of Zerubbabel and follows him through his journey to King Darius in Persia and his role in the Immemorial Discussion, as found in the apocryphal book, 1 Esdras. The purpose is to bridge the gap between Royal Arch Masonry and the Chivalric Orders as well as between the Old Testament and the New Testament. The Illustrious Order of the Red Cross teaches the lessons of the triumph of truth.

The Degree of Knight of St Paul (or Mediterranean Pass)

This degree is conferred as a prerequisite to becoming a Knight of Malta, in both the York Rite and independent 'stand-alone' versions of Knight Templar Freemasonry. The "Preliminary Declarations" of the Order of Malta ritual in England state of a candidate for the Order of Malta: "He must also have received the Degree of Knight of St Paul, including the Mediterranean Pass". The exact status of the 'Mediterranean Pass' has at times led to confusion as

Figure 29: *The Maltese Cross, symbol of the Order of Malta.*

to whether this is the 'stub' of a separate degree. The English ritual book clarified this in its 1989 edition (and subsequent editions) by stating: "The Mediterranean Pass is one of the secrets of the Degree of Knight of St Paul".[185]

This degree is close to being a true 'side degree', in that a small group (usually three) of members of the degree take the candidate "to one side" (i.e. apart on his own) and simply communicate the secrets of the degree to him, without actually working the ceremonial ritual of the degree. The only respect in which the degree fails to meet the definition of a true 'side degree' is that a Chapter of the Order is formally opened and closed by the presiding officer, on either side of the secrets being communicated.

The Degree of Knight of Malta (Order of Malta)

This degree is universally associated with the Masonic Knights Templar. In the York Rite system it is conferred before the Templar Degree; in the 'stand-alone' tradition it is conferred subsequently to the Templar Degree. It is known by varying degrees of formality as the *Order of Malta*, or the *Order of Knights of Malta*, or the *Ancient and Masonic Order of St John of Jerusalem, Palestine, Rhodes, and Malta*. In practice this last and fullest version of the name tends to be reserved to letterheads, rituals, and formal documents.

Figure 30: *The Cross and Crown, symbol of the Order of the Temple as found in the York Rite.*

The ceremony for conferring the degree (which is always worked in full) contains a mixture of masonic tradition, historical accounts of the Order of St John, moral teaching, and the communication of modes of recognition between members. A series of banners is employed in the ceremony, each representing one of the great battles of the historic medieval Order of St John, whose story is the basis of the moral teachings of the degree.

The Degree of Knight of the Temple (Order of the Temple)

The original medieval Order of Knights Templar was established after the First Crusade, and existed from approximately 1118 to 1312. There is no known historical evidence to link the medieval Knights Templar and Masonic Templarism, nor do the Masonic Knights Templar organizations claim any such direct link to the original medieval Templar organization.[186] Though it has been said that its affiliation with Masonry is based on texts that indicate persecuted Templars found refuge within the safety of Freemasonry, the order itself states that "there is no proof of direct connection between the ancient order and the modern order known today as the Knights Templar."[187] The official motto of the Knights Templar is In Hoc Signo Vinces, the rendition in Latin of the Greek phrase "εν τούτῳ νίκα", en toutōi nika, meaning "in this [sign] you will conquer".

Figure 31: *An American freemason in 2009.*

The Knight Templar degree is associated with elaborate regalia (costume) the precise detail of which varies between nations. The ritual draws upon the traditions of medieval Knights Templar, using them to impart moral instruction consistent with the biblical teachings of the Christian tradition.

Organization

In England and Wales, the teachings of the Order of the Red Cross feature in the *Red Cross of Babylon* which forms part of the Allied Masonic Degrees.

The Order of the Red Cross is often considered a compressed version of the Red Cross Degrees or Green Degrees which make up the Order of Knight Masons.

The Order of the Red Cross should not be confused with the Red Cross of Constantine.

Other Rites

Degrees of the York Rite in the United States

In the United States, a Knights Templar commandery is traditionally the final body that a member joins in the York Rite after the chapter of Royal Arch

Masons and a council of Royal & Select Masters. Some jurisdictions, however, allow members to skip over membership in a council. A local Knights Templar commandery operates under a state-level Grand Commandery, however American commanderies also operate under The Grand Encampment of the United States. This is less common among American Masonic bodies, as many report to the state level alone.

While a chapter bestows the Royal Arch degrees, and a council bestows the Cryptic degrees, a Knights Templar commandery bestows three orders and one preparatory degree onto its members. This is opposed to the standard degree system found elsewhere in Freemasonry, and they are the only ones not to deal with the Hiramic Legend.[188] The York Rite orders are:

- *The Illustrious Order of the Red Cross*
- *The Degree of Saint Paul* (or the Mediterranean Pass)
- *The Order of the Knights of Malta* (or simply *Order of Malta*)
- *The Order of the Temple*

Templar degrees in the Ancient and Accepted Scottish Rite

History and legend concerning the historical Knights Templar also play an important role in the degrees of the Ancient and Accepted Scottish Rite of Freemasonry, notably in the Rite's 30th Degree, Knight Kadosh. Other Scottish Rite degrees sometimes styled "Templar Degrees" include the 28th Degree (Knight Commander of the Temple, formerly denominated the 27th Degree in the Southern Jurisdiction of United States), the 29th Degree (Scottish Knight of Saint Andrew), the 32nd Degree (Master of the Royal Secret), and the 33rd Degree (Inspector General).[189]

Templar themes in wider Freemasonry

Despite Freemasonry's general disclaimer that no one Masonic organization claims a direct heritage to the medieval Knights Templar, certain degrees and orders are obviously patterned after the medieval Order. These are best described as "commemorative orders" or degrees. Nevertheless, in spite of the fraternity's official disclaimers, some Masons, non-Masons, and even anti-Masons insist that certain Masonic rites or degrees originally had direct Templar influence. Below are accounts of some of these theories and references.

- American Masonic youth organizations, such as the Order of DeMolay for young men, are named after the last Grand Master Templar Jacques de Molay, who was executed in the final suppression of the Templar order in the early 14th century.

- The Knight of Rose-Croix Degree in the "Ancient Accepted Scottish Rite", and honorary Orders like the Royal Order of Scotland are interpreted as evidence of a historical Templar-Masonic connection, though there is no factual basis for this belief.
- Rosslyn Chapel near Edinburgh has been suggested as evidence of a strong link between the Knights Templar and Freemasons; its reliefs are believed to express Templar and Freemason symbolism. But historian Dr. Louise Yeoman, along with other mediaeval scholars, says the Knights Templar connection is false. She notes that Rosslyn Chapel was built by William Sinclair so that Masses could be said for the souls of his family. In addition, the theory that Rosslyn Chapel is connected to Freemasonry or the Templars has been vigorously disputed by Robert L. D. Cooper, the Curator of the Grand Lodge of Scotland Museum and Library. It is postulated that any existing Masonic imagery was likely added at a later date, probably in the 1860s, when James St Clair-Erskine, 3rd Earl of Rosslyn instructed Edinburgh architect David Bryce, a known Freemason, to undertake restoration work on areas of the church, including many of the carvings.[190]
- Legends in certain degrees recount that Knights under the command of Sir John De Bermingham, first and last Earl of Louth, aided Scottish King Robert the Bruce, who had been excommunicated, at the Battle of Bannockburn;[191] but this account is based on an 18th-century romance and is not supported by any evidence. This story is the basis for the degrees in the Royal Order of Scotland, an invitational Masonic honorary organization.
- Templar connections have also been suggested through the Earls of Rosslyn (St. Clair, or Sinclair) a family with well-documented connections with Scottish Freemasonry, one being a Grand Master of the Grand Lodge of Scotland.
- Many other old and new organizations have taken the name of "Knights Templar". However, organizations such as the Order of the Solar Temple, Militi Templi Scotia, Ordo Templi Orientis, or the Sovereign Military Order of the Temple of Jerusalem are in no way related to Masonic Knights Templar, and share little or no relationship with it in history, hierarchy, or ritual.

References

Bibliography

- *The History Channel, Decoding the Past: The Templar Code*, 2005, video documentary

- *The History Channel, Mysteries of the Freemasons*, 2006 video documentary
- Stephen Dafoe, *The Compasses and the Cross*, 2008. ISBN 0-85318-298-1
- Gordon, Franck (2012). *The Templar Code: French title: Le Code Templier*. Paris, France: Yvelinedition. ISBN 978-2-84668-253-4.
- Christopher L. Hodapp and Alice Von Kannon, *The Templar Code For Dummies*, 2007. ISBN 0-470-12765-1
- Sean Martin, *The Knights Templar: History & Myths*, 2005. ISBN 1-56025-645-1
- http://news.bbc.co.uk/2/hi/uk_news/magazine/7050713.stm

External links

 Wikimedia Commons has media related to *Knights Templar (Freemasonry)*.

Masonic Knights Templar organizations

- Grand Encampment of Knights Templar of the United States of America[192]
- Sovereign Great Priory of the Knights Templar of Canada[193]
- Order of the Temple - Great Priory of Scotland[194]
- Order of the Temple - Great Priory of Ireland[195]
- Knights Templar Eye Foundation[196]
- The Web of Hiram[197] Section on The Royal Exalted Religious and Military Order of Masonic Knights Templar of England and Wales at Bradford University

Preceded by Holy Royal Arch	Knights Templar	Succeeded by Knights Templar Priest, Order of St. Thomas of Acon or Order of Knights Beneficent of the Holy City

Appendix

References

[1] Burman 1990, p. 45.
[2] //en.wikipedia.org/w/index.php?title=Template:Knights_Templar&action=edit
[3] Barber 1994.
[4] Martin 2005, p. 47.
[5] Nicholson 2001, p. 4.
[6] Barber 1993.
[7] Burman 1990, pp. 13, 19.
[8]
[9] Barber 1994, p. 7.
[10] Read 2001, p. 91.
[11] Burman 1990, p. 40.
[12]
[13] Martin 2005.
[14] Martin 2005, p. 99.
[15] Martin 2005, p. 113.
[16] Demurger, p. 139 "During four years, Jacques de Molay and his order were totally committed, with other Christian forces of Cyprus and Armenia, to an enterprise of reconquest of the Holy Land, in liaison with the offensives of Ghazan, the Mongol Khan of Persia."
[17] Nicholson 2001, p. 5.
[18] Nicholson 2001, p. 237.
[19] Barber 2006.
[20] Barber 1993, p. 178.
[21] Martin 2005, p. 118.
[22] Martin 2005, p. 122.
[23] Sobecki 2006, p. 963.
[24] Barber 1993, p. 3.
[25] Martin 2005, p. 123–24.
[26] Martin 2005, p. 125.
[27] Martin 2005, p. 140.
[28] Malcolm Barber has researched this legend and concluded that it originates from *La Chronique métrique attribuée à Geffroi de Paris*, ed. A. Divèrres, Strasbourg, 1956, pp. 5711–42. Geoffrey of Paris was "apparently an eye-witness, who describes de Molay as showing no sign of fear and, significantly, as telling those present that God would avenge their deaths".
[29] In *The New Knighthood* Barber referred to a variant of this legend, about how an unspecified Templar had appeared before and denounced Clement V and, when he was about to be executed sometime later, warned that both Pope and King would "within a year and a day be obliged to explain their crimes in the presence of God", found in the work by Ferretto of Vicenza, *Historia rerum in Italia gestarum ab anno 1250 ad annum usque 1318*
[30] Moeller 1912.
[31] José Vicente de Bragança, The Military Order of Christ and the Papal Croce di Cristo https://web.archive.org/web/20080506100231/http://jvarnoso.com/orders/christ2.html
[32] Martin 2005, pp. 140–42.
[33] Charles d' Aigrefeuille, *Histoire de la ville de Montpellier*, Volume 2, p. 193 (Montpellier: J. Martel, 1737–1739).
[34] Sophia Menache, *Clement V*, p. 218, 2002 paperback edition (Cambridge University Press, originally published in 1998).
[35] Germain-François Poullain de Saint-Foix, *Oeuvres complettes de M. de Saint-Foix, Historiographe des Ordres du Roi*, p. 287, Volume 3 (Maestricht: Jean-Edme Dupour & Philippe Roux, Imprimeurs-Libraires, associés, 1778).
[36] Étienne Baluze, *Vitae Paparum Avenionensis*, 3 Volumes (Paris, 1693).

[37] Pierre Dupuy, *Histoire de l'Ordre Militaire des Templiers* (Foppens, Brusselles, 1751).
[38] Burman 1990, p. 28.
[39] Barber 1993, p. 10.
[40] Barber 1994, p. 190.
[41] Martin 2005, p. 54.
[42] Read 2001, p. 137.
[43] Burman 1990, p. 43.
[44] Burman 1990, p. 30–33.
[45] Martin 2005, p. 32.
[46] Barber 1994, p. 191.
[47] Burman 1990, p. 44.
[48] (WT, 12.7, p. 554. James of Vitry, 'Historia Hierosolimatana', ed. J. ars, Gesta Dei per Francos, vol I(ii), Hanover, 1611, p. 1083, interprets this as a sign of martyrdom.)
[49] Burman 1990, p. 46.
[50] Nicholson 2001, p. 141.
[51] Barber 1994, p. 193.
[52] Nicholson 2001, pp. 48, 124–27.
[53] Martin 2005, p. 52.
[54] Barber 1993, p. 4.
[55] Martin 2005, p. 58.
[56] Barber 1994, pp. 194–95.
[57] *The Mythology Of The Secret Societies* (London: Secker and Warburg, 1972).
[58] Peter Partner, *The Murdered Magicians: The Templars And Their Myth* (Oxford: Oxford University Press, 1982).
[59] John Wallis, *Apocalyptic Trajectories: Millenarianism and Violence In The Contemporary World*, p. 130 (Bern: Peter Lang AG, European Academic Publishers, 2004).
[60] Michael Haag, *Templars: History and Myth: From Solomon's Temple To The Freemasons* (Profile Books Ltd, 2009).
[61] Knights Templar FAQ http://www.knightstemplar.org/faq.html#origin, accessed 10 January 2007.
[62] Louis Charpentier, *Les Mystères de la Cathédrale de Chartres* (Paris: Robert Laffont, 1966), translated *The Mysteries of Chartres Cathedral* (London: Research Into Lost Knowledge Organization, 1972).
[63] . Helmut Brackert, Stephan Fuchs (eds.), *Titurel*, Walter de Gruyter, 2002, p. 189 https://books.google.ch/books?id=6v224EoQ8Q4C&pg=PA189. There is no evidence of any actual connection of the historical Templars with the Grail, nor any claim on the part of any Templar to have discovered such a relig. See Karen Ralls, *Knights Templar Encyclopedia: The Essential Guide to the People, Places, Events and Symbols of the Order of the Temple*, p. 156 (The Career Press, Inc., 2007).
[64] http://www.lundyisleofavalon.co.uk/templars/tempic09.htm
[65] http://www.uthscsa.edu/mission/spring96/shroud.htm
[66] //doi.org/10.1016/j.jmedhist.2004.03.004
[67] https://web.archive.org/web/20081002212952/http://www.renaissancemagazine.com/backissues/templar.html
[68] https://www.renaissancemagazine.com/backissues/templar.html
[69] https://www.imdb.com/title/tt0843844/
[70] https://www.dominicselwood.com/the-knights-templar-1-the-knights
[71] https://www.dominicselwood.com/the-knights-templars-2-sergeants-chaplains-women-affiliates
[72] https://www.dominicselwood.com/birth-of-the-order
[73] https://www.dominicselwood.com/the-knights-templar-4-st-bernard-of-clairvaux
[74] https://www.bbkl.de/public/index.php/frontend/lexicon?letter=M&child=Ma&article=marigny_p.art
[75] htpps//www.academia.edu
[76] http://www.sacred-texts.com/sro/hkt/index.htm
[77] http://visualiseur.bnf.fr/ark:/12148/bpt6k91414v

[78] http://www.slate.com/id/2140307/
[79] https://curlie.org/Society/Religion_and_Spirituality/Esoteric_and_Occult/Templars/
[80] Janetta Rebold Benton, *Materials, methods, and masterpieces of medieval art*, p. 257 (Greenwood Publishing Group, 2009).
[81] *Knights Templar: Protectors of the Holy Grail*, video documentary on the National Geographic Channel, February 22, 2006, written by Jesse Evans
[82] Richard the Lionheart and the Knights Templar http://www.masonicsourcebook.com/king_richard_lionheart_knights_templar.htm Charles Greenstreet Addison, *The History of the Knights Templars*, 1842, pp. 141–49.
[83] (referenced in Kahn's *Codebreakers*)
[84] The History Channel, *Decoding the Past: The Templar Code*, video documentary, November 7, 2005, written by Marcy Marzuni
[85] Gary Lachman, *Politics and the Occult: The Left, the Right, and the Radically Unseen*, p. 41 (Quest Books, 2008).
[86] Sean Martin, *The Knights Templar: History & Myths*, 2005.
[87] *Lost Worlds: Knights Templar*, July 10, 2006, video documentary on *The History Channel*
[88] Julien Théry, "A Heresy of State : Philip the Fair, the Trial of the 'Perfidious Templars', and the Ponticalization of the French Monarchy", *Journal of Religious Medieval Cultures* 39/2 (2013), pp. 117–48
[89] https://archive.org/stream/historyofinquis03leah#page/262/mode/2up Vol. III Chpt. 5 par 2. Not in Copyright
[90] The Trial of the Knights Templar, Malcolm Barbor, 1978
[91] Les Templiers, une chevalerie chrétienne au moyen-âge, Alain Demurger
[92] Barbor, Malcolm. The Trial of the Templars. 1978 p. 178 para 1 p. 179 para. 1.
[93] Martin, p. 118.
[94] Malcolm Barber, *The Trial of the Templars*, 2nd edn. (Cambridge, 2006), pp. 2, 217–58; also see Anne Gilmour-Bryson, *The Trial of the Templars in Cyprus*, (Leiden, 1998).
[95] Gordon Napier, *The Rise and Fall of the Knights Templar*, 2003.
[96] Processus Cypricus (SchottmiiUcr, II. 379, 382, 383).*Procfes, L 404 ; IL 260, 281, 284, 295, 299, 338, 354, 356, 363, 389, 390, 395, 407.—Bini, pp. 468, 488
[97] Norman Cohn, *Europe's Inner Demons – The Demonization of Christians In Medieval Christendom*. (Pimlico, revised 1993 edition).
[98] Barber, *Trial of the Templars*, pp. 209–13.
[99] Charles Raymond Dillon, *Templar Knights and the Crusades*, p. 164 (iUniverse Books, 2005).
[100] Karen Ralls, *Knights Templar Encyclopedia: The Essential Guide to The People, Places, Events, and Symbols of The Order of The Temple*, p. 153 (The Career Press, Inc., 2007).
[101] Karen Ralls, page 154
[102] Evelyn Lord, *The Templar's Curse*, p. 137 (Pearson Education Limited, 2008).
[103] Barbara Frale, 'The Chinon Chart: Papal Absolution to the last Templar, Master Jacques de Molay', *Journal of Medieval History*, 30 (2004), 127.
[104] Karen Ralls, *Knights Templar Encyclopedia: The Essential Guide to the People, Places, Events, and Symbols of the Order of the Temple* (New Page Books, 2007).
[105] Hugh J. Schonfield, *The Essene Odyssey*. Longmead, Shaftesbury, Dorset SP7 8BP, England: Element Books Ltd., 1984; 1998 paperback reissue, p. 164.
[106] The History of the Knights Templar, Temple Church and the Temple, by Charles G. Addison, Esq., London, pp. 196, 350, not in copyright, available thru the Internet Archives gateway.
[107] Malcolm Barber, *The New Knighthood: A History of the Order of the Temple* (Cambridge University Press, 1993).
[108] *Processus Contra Templarios*, Exemplaria Praetiosa, published on 25 October 2007.
[109] Charles d' Aigrefeuille, *Histoire de la ville de Montpellier*, Volume 2, p. 193 (Montpellier: J. Martel, 1737–1739).
[110] Sophia Menache, *Clement V*, p. 218, 2002 paperback edition (Cambridge University Press, originally published in 1998).
[111] Germain-François Poullain de Saint-Foix, *Oeuvres complettes de M. De Saint-Foix, Historiographe des Ordres du Roi*, p. 287, Volume 3 (Maestricht: Jean-Edme Dupour & Philippe Roux, Imprimeurs-Libraires, associés, 1778).

[112] Étienne Baluze, *Vitae Paparum Avenionensis*, 3 Volumes (Paris, 1693).
[113] Pierre Dupuy, *Histoire de l'Ordre Militaire des Templiers* (Foppens, Brusselles, 1751).
[114] https//archive.is
[115] https//www.academia.edu
[116] http://www.newadvent.org/cathen/14493a.htm
[117] http://www.templarhistory.com/
[118] http://www.templarsinslovakia.com/
[119] http://www.ourcatholicfaith.org/confession.html
[120] http://www.SCMOTH1804OSMTJ.ORG/
[121] Helen Nicholson, *The Proceedings Against the Templars in the British Isles*, Volume 2, page 5 (Ashgate Publishing: 2011).
[122] Helen Nicholson, *The Proceedings Against the Templars in the British Isles*, Volume 2, page 6 (Ashgate Publishing: 2011).
[123] Barbara Frale, "The Chinon Chart: Papal absolution to the last Templar, Master Jacques de Molay" (*Journal of Medieval History*, Volume 30, issue 2 [June, 2004], p. 128).
[124] *Processus Contra Templarios*, Exemplaria Praetiosa, published on October 25, 2007.
[125] Barbara Frale, "The Chinon Chart: Papal absolution to the last Templar, Master Jacques de Molay" (*Journal of Medieval History*, Volume 30, issue 2 [June, 2004], p. 125).
[126] Anne Gilmour-Bryson explored this issue at length in her article, "Sodomy and the Knights Templar" (*Journal of the History of Sexuality* 7:2 [October 1996], pp. 151-183). She begins her inquiry with the warning that, "In any examination of Inquisition testimony, it is impossible to lay aside the effect that torture must have had on the answers given." (p. 153).
[127] Gordon Napier, *The Rise and Fall of the Knights Templar*.
[128] The vagueness of the term *sodomy*, applied to all sexual acts that did not lead directly to procreation, is explored in John Boswell, *Christianity, Social Tolerance, and Homosexuality* (1980).
[129] Barbara Frale, "The Chinon Chart: Papal absolution to the last Templar, Master Jacques de Molay" (*Journal of Medieval History*, Volume 30, issue 2 [June, 2004], pages 109-134).
[130] Barbara Frale, *Il Papato e il processo ai Templari: L'inedita assoluzione di Chinon alla luce della diplomatica pontificia* (Viella, 2002).
[131] Charles d' Aigrefeuille, *Histoire de la ville de Montpellier*, Volume 2, page 193 (Montpellier: J. Martel, 1737-1739).
[132] Sophia Menache, *Clement V*, page 218, 2002 paperback edition (Cambridge University Press, originally published in 1998).
[133] Germain-François Poullain de Saint-Foix, *Oeuvres complettes de M. De Saint-Foix, Historiographe des Ordres du Roi*, page 287, Volume 3 (Maestricht: Jean-Edme Dupour & Philippe Roux, Imprimeurs-Libraires, associés, 1778).
[134] Étienne Baluze, *Vitae Paparum Avenionensis*, 3 Volumes (Paris, 1693).
[135] Pierre Dupuy, *Histoire de l'Ordre Militaire des Templiers* (Foppens, Brusselles, 1751).
[136] https://dx.doi.org/10.1016/j.jmedhist.2004.03.004
[137] http://asv.vatican.va/en/pers/personale/Barbara_Frale.htm
[138] https://web.archive.org/web/20060101174727/http://www.mulino.it/edizioni/foreign_rights/backlist/history/frale.htm
[139] https://web.archive.org/web/20071011034616/http://asv.vatican.va/en/doc/1308.htm
[140] http://asv.vatican.va/en/doc/1308.htm
[141] http://www.inrebus.com/chinon.php
[142] //en.wikipedia.org/w/index.php?title=Template:Knights_Templar&action=edit
[143] Fulk after entrusting his county of Anjou to Henry II, King of England about 1119, had gone to Jerusalem where Orderic Vitalis states that he "attached himself for some time to the Knights of the Temple". Fulk returned to Anjou probably in the latter half of 1121 (The Laud Chronicle 1121 in "The Anglo-Saxon Chronicles")
[144] http://libro.uca.edu/forey/templars.htm
[145] http://www.british-history.ac.uk/report.aspx?compid=36281#n6
[146] Jean Richard, "The adventure of John Gale, knight of Tyre", in *The Experience of Crusading*, vol. 1, ed. Jonathan Riley-Smith, Peter W. Edbury, Jonathan P. Phillips, p. 195, n. 26
[147] Malcolm Barber, *The New Knighthood*, p. 353, n. 120.
[148] Excerpta Historica, Samuel Bentley Pub. 1831

[149] http://www.templiers.org/richerenches.php
[150] La Commanderie du Ruou http://commanderieduruou.free.fr/commandruou15b.html
[151] Templiers des Ardennes http://templiers-ardennes.fr.tc/
[152] Dobronić, Lelja, Templari i ivanovci u Hrvatskoj, p. 77
[153] Magyar Országos Levéltár
[154] Died in Prison in Kyrenia in 1316. *Chroniques d'Amadi et de Stambaldi*, ed. Rene de Mas Latrie, Collection de documents inedits, 2 vols. (Paris, 1891–1893) p. 398
[155] Templar Route http://www.templariusze.org/templarroute/templarroute.htm
[156] https://books.google.com/books?id=7PJBAAAAcAAJ&pg=PA9&redir_esc=y#v=onepage&q&f=false Memorias E Noticias Historicas Da Celebre Ordem Militar dos Templarios – Para a História da admirável da Ordem de Nosso Senhor Jesus Cristo, Alexandre Ferreira, 1735 (pp. 720, 750–52, 1032) (Portuguese, Latin)
[157] https://books.google.com/books?id=fRkbAAAAYAAJ&pg=PA1&redir_esc=y André Jean Paraschi, 1990, Sol Invinctus atelier (pp. 10–)
[158] //en.wikipedia.org/w/index.php?title=Template:Knights_Templar&action=edit
[159] //en.wikipedia.org/w/index.php?title=Template:Catholic_Church_hierarchy_sidebar&action=edit
[160] Armand de Périgord was either killed or captured at the battle of La Forbie; authorities differ. Richard de Bures commanded the Templars until the election of Guillaume de Sonnac; whether he was Grand Master is disputed. See Armand de Perigord (1178-1247), at www.templiers.org http://www.templiers.org/armandperigord.php
[161] //en.wikipedia.org/w/index.php?title=Template:Knights_Templar&action=edit
[162] Hyères http://pinterest.com/franceprovence/hyeres/, Pinterest, accessed 7 August 2013
[163] http://www.libdeau.fr/
[164] http://www.lechateaudelacouvertoirade.com
[165] News and Events, Keele University. Accessed 16 October 2014.
[166] http://www.ourcountrychurch.co.uk
[167] http://www.irishmasonichistory.com/the-knights-templar-and-ireland.html
[168] Vignette (top): The parable of the Good Samaritan. Vignettes (clockwise from bottom): "First drink - social. Second drink at a bar. Drinking & gambling. Goes home drunk to young wife. Pawns his clothes. Poverty & delirium. Recovery - signs the pledge. Prosperity & happy home."
[169] History of IOGT http://www.iogt.us/iogt.php?p=35, Derek Rutherford, National Council, USA
[170] Schmidt, Alvin J. *Fraternal Organizations* Westport, CT; Greenwood Press pp.147-8
[171] Schmidt p.147
[172] http://www.iogt.org/index.asp?id=139&thread=139&box=139
[173] http://www.iogt.pl
[174] http://www.iogt.org/
[175] http://www.glmmm.com/kt/default.aspx
[176] Pietre-Stones Biography of Ramsay http://www.freemasons-freemasonry.com/ramsay_biography_oration.html retrieved 22 June 2012
[177] Berne Manuscript http://reunir.free.fr/fm/rituels/berne.htm(French text)
[178] Karl Gotthelf von Hund und Altengrotkau German Wikipedia retrieved 26 July 2012
[179] The Temple and the Lodge, M. Baigent and R. Leigh, Arrow 1998, p264-267
[180] Irish Masonic Jewels http://www.irishmasonicjewels.ie/intro_topic220.html The Order of the Temple, A History, retrieved 26 July 2012
[181] History of Great Priory of Scotland http://www.greatprioryofscotland.com/history.htm retrieved 26 July 2012
[182] Masonic Dictionary http://www.masonicdictionary.com/templarh.html retrieved 26 July 2012
[183] William James Hughan, Unpublished Records of the Craft, Kenning, 1871, part II, pp 16-17
[184] issuu.com http://issuu.com/gektusa/docs/0111 Dr. Susan Mitchell Sommers, The Revival of a Patriotic Order: Knights Templar in England and New York, Knight Templar Magazine, 2 January 2011, retrieved 2 November 2012
[185] Great Priory Ritual No 2, The Ancient & Masonic Order of St John of Jerusalem, Palestine, Rhodes, and Malta (published 1989, London), page 3.
[186] Knights Templar FAQ/INFO http://www.knightstemplar.org/faq.html Accessed 14 August 2007

[187] http://www.knightstemplar.org/faq.html#origin [Knights Templar FAQ - Origin]
[188] http://www.knightstemplar.org/faq.html#member [Knights Templar FAQ - How to Become a Knight Templar]
[189] http://www.houstonscottishrite.org/wp-content/uploads/2013/04/Templar-Degrees-of-the-SR-v3.pdf, by Pierre G. Normand, Jr., 33°, retrieved 26 March 2013
[190] Michael T R B Turnbull, *Rosslyn Chapel Revealed* (review and synopsis) http://www.corbie.com/Books/rosslyn-chapel.html, Fort Augustus Abbey School Old Boys Association, accessed 8 May 2017
[191] Nolan, *History Journal*, 1988-89 https://web.archive.org/web/20060908070508/http://www.loyno.edu/history/journal/1988-9/nolan.htm
[192] http://www.knightstemplar.org
[193] http://www.knightstemplar.ca
[194] http://www.greatprioryofscotland.com
[195] http://freemason.ie/about-grand-lodge/appendant-bodies/great-priory-of-ireland/
[196] http://knightstemplar.org/ktef/
[197] http://www.brad.ac.uk/webofhiram/?section=masonic_knights_templar

Article Sources and Contributors

The sources listed for each article provide more detailed licensing information including the copyright status, the copyright owner, and the license conditions.

Knights Templar *Source:* https://en.wikipedia.org/w/index.php?oldid=854160017 *License:* Creative Commons Attribution-Share Alike 3.0 *Contributors:* 72, Aaronl113, Acroterion, Adam Bishop, Aledownload, AntiCompositeNumber, Anupam, Arado, Baydaneza, Besillica, Blanche of King's Lynn, BrownHairedGirl, Budhen, Bugatti35racer, CLCStudent, Carminowe of Hendra, Chewings72, Chicbyaccident, Classicwiki, ClueBot NG, CommonsDelinker, Crito10, Dane, Darthkenobi0, Dbachmann, Dcirovic, Diablo372, Dilidor, Dlohcierekim, Donner60, DrKay, Drewmutt, Dweller, ESND, Empmmus, Eric-Wester, Ericoides, Favonian, Felix558, Ferrdann, Finnusertop, Firsteleventh, FlightTime, FriyMan, Fugitron, Gilliam, Glancing Ocean 59, Gogo Dodo, GrazahXxX, GrindtXX, H.dryad, HaHaHaHa1, Hddty., Hmains, Hugo999, Ian.thomson, IronGargoyle, Jim1138, Jmg38, JoJan, John Cline, KH-1, Kablammo, Kansas Bear, Knightstemplar1889, KylieTastic, Laszlo Panaflex, Lindsay H, Magioladitis, Marcocapelle, Marek69, MarginalCost, Marvellous Spider-Man, Materialscientist, Maximajorian Viridio, Mckaysalisbury, Michaelbellino, Morningstar1814, Mutt Lunker, Natty10000, Nikkimaria, Ninth-Templar, Nøkkenbruer, Ontarioboy, Oshwah, PKT, Parkwells, Pauli133, Paxton Campbell, PeRshGo, ProprioMe OW, Red dwarf, Rhallanger, Rickraptor707, Rkcora, Robbor288, RobertG, SMcCandlish, Sadin Hussahd, Salix alba, Sangdeboeuf, Satellizer, Serafart, Serols, Shellwood, Shuipzv3, Soupforone, Srich32977, Sylas, The Rambling Man, TheGoodBadWorst, Thetruchairman, Thor Dockweiler, Torontino, Vale da Avalon, Victor24122, Vif12vf, Vincedumond, Wikipelli, Williamgarcia56, XPTO, Xphilosopherking, Xuzsagon, Yeryry, Yopie, Zacwill, Zyxw, Ранко Николић, 175 anonymous edits 1

History of the Knights Templar *Source:* https://en.wikipedia.org/w/index.php?oldid=852558807 *License:* Creative Commons Attribution-Share Alike 3.0 *Contributors:* Acroterion, Adam Bishop, Alansohn, Andy M. Wang, Appl044, Arthena, Auntof6, Avatar008, BD2412, BMRR, Barek, Belfire, Bender235, Berthold Werner, Bluebour, Camdic, Cannolis, Cgt, Charles Matthews, Chewings72, Chris the speller, ClueBot NG, CommonsDelinker, DASL51984, Dbachmann, Donner60, Ducknish, EKindig, Elonka, Empirecoins, English1123, Eric Hoogland, Ewa Bender, EyeKnows, Frosted14, Gfrago, GirasoleDE, Godot13, HaeB, Hmains, Iridescent, Jevansen, John "Hannibal" Smith, KH-1, Kaar9012, Kendrick7, Ketiltrout, Khazar2, Kibi78704, Klbrain, Lovkal, Lung salad, LuzoGraal, MSJapan, MZMcBride, Magioladitis, Marcocapelle, Materialscientist, McSly, Meaghan, Mikalra, Mild Bill Hiccup, Mogism, MrBill3, Mugginsx, NTox, Nikkimaria, Ninjaexpert2, Ninth-Templar, Ohnoitsjamie, Onel5969, Oshwah, Philip Trueman, Plasticspork, R'n'B, Raul654, Rhinestone K, Rocketrod1960, ScreaminXeagle, Seahorseruler, Shellwood, Snowolf, Srich32977, Sselbor, Stormarm, Str1977, Stryn, Tentinator, The Sage of Stamford, TheHamburger, Thucyd, Tom.Reding, Tpbradbury, Trilobitealive, Ucucha, Ulric1313, Vanity500, Wayne Slam, Widr, Woohookitty, Wtmitchell, XPTO, Xenwax, Yopie, Zinn2013, 192 anonymous edits 23

Chinon Parchment *Source:* https://en.wikipedia.org/w/index.php?oldid=853747871 *License:* Creative Commons Attribution-Share Alike 3.0 *Contributors:* Aelfthrytha, Attilios, Belfire, Bellerophon5685, Ben Ben, Bgwhite, Brandonrush, Caerwine, Charles Matthews, Chris the speller, ChrisGualtieri, Citation bot 1, Coemgenus, Corwin8, Dalgetty, Denniscabrams, Deses, Dr mindbender, Durova, Eeditress, Elonka, Error, Faithlessthewonderboy, Fatoprofugus, Ferengi, Firstorm, Geoffspear, Hmains, Hmainsbot1, Hu12, Iprocomp, Iridescent, JayHenry, Leandrod, Leszek Jańczuk, Loremaster, Lung salad, Marcocapelle, Meco, Motaka, Mugginsx, PeRshGo, SeanNovack, Silverwhistle, Skizzik, TheConductor, Thincat, Thucyd, TreasuryTag, Varlaam, Vik-Thor, Voyaging, Vyselink, WLRoss, Wareh, Wednesday Next, Wetman, Wikianon, Yopie, 31 anonymous edits 39

List of Knights Templar *Source:* https://en.wikipedia.org/w/index.php?oldid=846147948 *License:* Creative Commons Attribution-Share Alike 3.0 *Contributors:* Academic Challenger, Adam Bishop, Adam124, Aymatth2, Barek, Bender235, Bobby38takeajoke, Budija, Businessman332211, Cannolis, Charles Matthews, Chris the speller, ClueBot NG, Colonies Chris, Cydebot, Darren1900, Dragovit, Durova, Edgemaniac, Elonka, Emilliannno, Empello, Farkasven, GalaazV, General Ization, Giadrome, Gpazpujalt, GregorB, Greyman, Haleghton, Hmains, Hugo999, JASpencer, Jaffaquake, Jaques de Molays, Jeremy Bolwell, Jmccormac, John of Reading, Jugbo, Kkblank71, Kcordina, Khazar, Light Warrior, LindsayH, Lordknowle, Loremaster, Luvmel316, LuzoGraal, MER-C, Mazdabomb, MichaelMaggs, Mugginsx, Nikkimaria, None but shining hours, Nsaa, Oculi, Oluwa2Chainz, Pearle, Pedrovq, Pheeboris, Plucas58, Rich Farmbrough, Rillian, Salvadorjo∼enwiki, Skydiver15000, Srich32977, Srnec, Str1977, Szwedzki, T-dot, Tajotep, The Ogre, Tide rolls, Tlf-t4pa, Torontino, Wai Hong, Walter9, Wiki alf, Wjhonson, XPTO, Yopie, Zzuuzz, 231 anonymous edits 45

Grand Masters of the Knights Templar *Source:* https://en.wikipedia.org/w/index.php?oldid=835889510 *License:* Creative Commons Attribution-Share Alike 3.0 *Contributors:* 11dragon11, Adam Bishop, Alaniaris, AlexWelens, Alfreddo, Andrew Dalby, AnonMoos, Bender235, Charlik, Chicbyaccident, ClueBot NG, Codenamecuckoo, CommonsDelinker, Cplakidas, ChristianCita, Deliogul, Dragovit, Durova, Elonka, Epicgenius, Geekdiva, Gilliam, Gregakapun, Greyman, Grye, Heracletus, Hmains, Jmccormac, Joefromrandb, Kcordina, Kiril Simeonovski, LQEngineer, Lars Y., Lordknowle, Lquilter, MadGuy7023, Marco Antonio Sotomorin, Nabla, Nikkimaria, Pmanderson, R107, Ragnarriolfbrok, S@bre, SMP, Sadalmia, Snowolf, Str1977, Studegar, Sundostund, Tabor, Tajotep, Tefalstar, The Catholic Knight, The Ogre, The Traditionalist, Tlf-t4pa, Tuckerresearch, Vincedumond, Zzuuzz, Максим Підтиснов, 73 anonymous edits 61

List of Knights Templar sites *Source:* https://en.wikipedia.org/w/index.php?oldid=853838826 *License:* Creative Commons Attribution-Share Alike 3.0 *Contributors:* AbeVartach, Aguyanon, AlphaMikeFoxtrot, Andronicus92, Angusmclellan, Aquilanus, Balantrodach, Baron Liscreagh, Baronnet, Bgwhite, Blanche of King's Lynn, Boris Živ, Brendandh, Budija, CW - U.T., Carewiser, Charles Matthews, Chicbyaccident, Climent Sostres, ClueBot NG, DavisGL, Dbachmann, DiverScout, Dpaajones, Edgemaniac, Edward321, Elonka, Emilliannno, EverythingGeography, Gandalf33, Gjs2238, Gocherj, Headbomb, Invicta21, Itsmejudith, Jack1956, Jezzabr, Kebeta, Khazar2, L'honorable, Legobot II, Leutha, Liam McCauley, LilHelpa, Lordknowle, Loremaster, LouisAlain, LuzoGraal, M-le-mot-dit, Marcelivan, MarcusVeus, Masterofmydomains, Millbanks, Mmurray2, Mogism, Nedrutland, Nick Number, Oliviaowen, Olivier, OpenFuture, Out90, PamD, Pedrovq, Peter Ellis, Plucas58, Ptbotgourou, Raulgh, Rodw, Rory Elkinson, Rushton2010, S@bre, SchreiberBike, Shawn in Montreal, Shpoffo, Simon Burchell, Sisswrn, Slightsmile, Stephane787∼enwiki, Mascusine, Tajotep, Technolalia, Ubav, Ulf Heinsohn, Utility Monster, Vieque, VoABot II, Vvven, WOSlinker, WRK, Walter9, XPTO, Xover, Yopie, Zxconcept, 126 anonymous edits 67

International Organisation of Good Templars *Source:* https://en.wikipedia.org/w/index.php?oldid=846506500 *License:* Creative Commons Attribution-Share Alike 3.0 *Contributors:* Addicted2Sanity, Anna Smelova, Bellerophon5685, Blathnaid, Bmbaker88, Böri, Caerwine, Chairboy, ClueBot NG, Cuchullain, David Justin, Deadbeef, Domino theory, Doncram, Fuhghettaboutit, GeneralMelchett, Geniac, Good Olfactory, Gordonofcartoon, Gr55tay, Hmains, Hugo999, J heisenberg, Jmabel, Johnpacklambert, Jorunn, Kintetsubuffalo, Linuxbeak, Lquilter, Mahlum∼enwiki, Marek69, Mikael Hansson, Mu, NatusRoma, Nihiltres, Nunquam Dormio, Pfa, Plrk, Pointlessforest, RHaworth, Rapsar, Scarpy, SimonP, SoberFreeman, SummerPhD, TAnthony, Topbanana, Valfontis, 31 anonymous edits 73

Knights Templar (Freemasonry) *Source:* https://en.wikipedia.org/w/index.php?oldid=854000096 *License:* Creative Commons Attribution-Share Alike 3.0 *Contributors:* 2D, A Great Catholic Person, Aaron816, Alansohn, Annetromney, Aoidh, Appl04, Av99, BD2412, Banaticus, Barek, Berengaria, Besillica, BlueTemplar13, Bluebour, Booooooom, Bruno P. Ramos, Chicbyaccident, Claofom Soluis, ClueBot NG, Croquen, Cruithneach77, Cyan22, Darkwind, Dbachmann, Diannaa, Dl2000, Doug Weller, Drudgeon, EFKnappAV, Eeekster, Elonka, Faustus37, Fiddlersmouth, Gadget850, Gilliam, GrapedApe, GreenReaper, Grye, HandsomeFella, Heirx, Hmains, ImprovementUK, IronGargoyle, Jezzabr, Joe Decker (alt), John of Reading, JohnSawyer, KH-1, Kerrykaye, LakesideMiners, Lmateo002, Lung salad, MB, MSJapan, Maestro79∼enwiki, Marasmusine, Marcocapelle, Mason Watcher, Micahtheangel, Montagu 1234, Moxy, Mpk138, Mptp94, Mugginsx, Myland, NamelsRon, Ndg.2010, Neilbeach, Nerodog, Nick Number, PGNormand, Parkwells, PeRshGo, Philip Trueman, Pragmaticstatistic, ProfKay, RFM57, RSStockdale, Rich Farmbrough, RiverStyx23, Rjwilmsi, Robofish, SGT141, Snozzer, Soltaran, Soupforone, StarlitGlitter, Subash.chandran007, Sukiari, The Letter J, The wub, Timothy Titus, Tom harrison, Tomdo08, TwinsMetsFan, Tymblade, Vaastuvit, Waggers, Wiki alf, Woohookitty, Yamamoto Ichiro, Zef, 143 anonymous edits 79

97

Image Sources, Licenses and Contributors

The sources listed for each image provide more detailed licensing information including the copyright status, the copyright owner, and the license conditions.

Image *Source:* https://en.wikipedia.org/w/index.php?title=File:Seal_of_Templars.jpg *License:* Public Domain *Contributors:* Thomas Andrew Archer, Charles Lethbridge Kingsford 1

Image *Source:* https://en.wikipedia.org/w/index.php?title=File:Cross_of_the_Knights_Templar.svg *License:* Public domain *Contributors:* User:Kbolino 2

Image *Source:* https://en.wikipedia.org/w/index.php?title=File:Flag_of_the_Order_of_St._John_(various).svg *License:* Public domain *Contributors:* Alaspada, Benzoyl, Cathy Richards, Continentaleurope, Dancer, Ec.Domnowall, Fschoenm, G.dallorto, Gödeke, Hamelin de Guettelet, Homo lupus, Hydrargyrum, Joostik, Kahusi, McSush, Mnmazur, Oren neu dag, Paul2, Perhelion, Piotrus, Sarang, Thomas81, Zscout370, Ранко Николић 3

Image *Source:* https://en.wikipedia.org/w/index.php?title=File:Flag_of_Portugal.svg *License:* Public Domain *Contributors:* Columbano Bordalo Pinheiro (1910; generic design); Vítor Luís Rodrigues; António Martins-Tuválkin (2004; this specific v 3

Image *Source:* https://en.wikipedia.org/w/index.php?title=File:Flag_of_the_Vatican_City.svg *License:* Public Domain *Contributors:* AguaitantPV~commonswiki, Cathy Richards, Consta, Cycn, DenghiùComm, Denniss, Durin, F l a n k e r, Fry1989, Fulvio314, GoldenRainbow, HoheHoffnungen, Homo lupus, InfattiVedeteCheViDice, Jarekt, Jed, Klemen Kocjancic, Krun, Liftarn, Ludger1961, Mattes, Next2u, NielsF, Nightstallion, OAlexander~commonswiki, P-JR, Pumbaa80, RainbowSilver2ndBackup, Ravenpuff, Ricordisamoa, Robin van der Vliet, SiBr4, Steinsplitter, Str4nd, TFerenczy, Tacsipacsi, WikiDan61, Zscout370, Эрманарих, علی المزارقه, 22 anonymous edits 3

Image *Source:* https://en.wikipedia.org/w/index.php?title=File:Flag_of_Spain.svg *License:* Public Domain *Contributors:* Anomie, Jo-Jo Eumerus, Topbanana 3

Image *Source:* https://en.wikipedia.org/w/index.php?title=File:046CupolaSPietro.jpg *License:* Creative Commons Attribution-Sharealike 3.0 *Contributors:* MarkusMark 3

Figure 1 *Source:* https://en.wikipedia.org/w/index.php?title=File:Bandeira_Templária.svg *Contributors:* User:Rkcora 4

Figure 2 *Source:* https://en.wikipedia.org/w/index.php?title=File:Temple_mount.JPG *License:* GNU Free Documentation License *Contributors:* Auntof6, Berthold Werner, BotMultichillT, Chesdovi, Cnyborg, GeorgHH, Hobo Lifting Aroma, Judithcomm, OgreBot 2, Yonderboy, 3 anonymous edits 5

Figure 3 *Source:* https://en.wikipedia.org/w/index.php?title=File:Battle_of_Cresson.jpg *License:* Public Domain *Contributors:* Adam Bishop, AndreasPraefcke, Andrew Dalby, Asclepias, Cwbm (commons), Dragovit, Jcb, Jheald, Jianhui67, Kirill Lokshin, Ruslik0, Shakko, Túrelio, Un1c0s bot~commonswiki, Wieralee, 8 anonymous edits 7

Figure 4 *Source:* https://en.wikipedia.org/w/index.php?title=File:Tomar-Convento_de_Cristo-Rotunda_dos_Templários-20140914.jpg *Contributors:* Daniel VILLAFRUELA. 9

Figure 5 *Source:* https://en.wikipedia.org/w/index.php?title=File:Templars_on_Stake.jpg *License:* Public Domain *Contributors:* Bukk, Cirt, Finanzer, G.dallorto, Jibi44, Mattes, Schimmelreiter, Shakko, Tangopaso, 1 anonymous edits 10

Figure 6 *Source:* https://en.wikipedia.org/w/index.php?title=File:Chapelletemplier.jpg *License:* Creative Commons Attribution-ShareAlike 3.0 Unported *Contributors:* User:Zusammen030378~commonswiki 12

Figure 7 *Source:* https://en.wikipedia.org/w/index.php?title=File:Saint-Martin-des-Champs_Chapelle.JPG *License:* GNU Free Documentation License *Contributors:* Bohème, Chabe01, Kurpfalzbilder.de, MGA73bot2, Moonik, Reinhardhauke, Scorpius59, Thor19, Underwaterbuffalo, 1 anonymous edits 13

Figure 8 *Source:* https://en.wikipedia.org/w/index.php?title=File:HPIM3597.JPG *License:* Creative Commons Attribution 3.0 *Contributors:* JoJan 15

Figure 9 *Source:* https://en.wikipedia.org/w/index.php?title=File:Templari_Paris.jpg *License:* Public Domain *Contributors:* Acoma, Dbachmann, Jheald 16

Figure 10 *Source:* https://en.wikipedia.org/w/index.php?title=File:TempleChurch-Exterior.jpg *License:* Public domain *Contributors:* AlanFord 17

Image *Source:* https://en.wikipedia.org/w/index.php?title=File:Wikisource-logo.svg *License:* Creative Commons Attribution-Sharealike 3.0 *Contributors:* ChrisiPK, Guillom, INeverCry, Jarekt, JuTa, Leyo, Lokal Profil, MichaelMaggs, NielsF, Rei-artur, Rocket000, Romaine, Steinsplitter 19

Image *Source:* https://en.wikipedia.org/w/index.php?title=File:Commons-logo.svg *License:* logo *Contributors:* Anomie, Callanecc, CambridgeBayWeather, Jo-Jo Eumerus, RHaworth 21

Image *Source:* https://en.wikipedia.org/w/index.php?title=File:Cscr-featured.svg *License:* GNU Lesser General Public License *Contributors:* Anomie 21

Figure 11 *Source:* https://en.wikipedia.org/w/index.php?title=File:Templars_Burning.jpg *License:* Public Domain *Contributors:* AndreasPraefcke, Andrew Gray, Bohème, Butko, Darsie, Elonka, G.dallorto, Jheald, Jibi44, Johnbod, Judithcomm, Lotje, Mattes, Mel22, Moeby1, Olivier, Paris 16, Pline, Quibik, Shakko, Siren-Com, Thuresson, Un1c0s bot~commonswiki, 1 anonymous edits 24

Figure 12 *Source:* https://en.wikipedia.org/w/index.php?title=File:KnightsTemplarPlayingChess1283.jpg *License:* Public Domain *Contributors:* Alphonse le Sage (Alfonso X) 26

Figure 13 *Source:* https://en.wikipedia.org/w/index.php?title=File:Battle_of_Cresson.jpg *License:* Public Domain *Contributors:* Adam Bishop, AndreasPraefcke, Andrew Dalby, Asclepias, Cwbm (commons), Dragovit, Jcb, Jheald, Jianhui67, Kirill Lokshin, Ruslik0, Shakko, Túrelio, Un1c0s bot~commonswiki, Wieralee, 8 anonymous edits 27

Figure 14 *Source:* https://en.wikipedia.org/w/index.php?title=File:Papst_klemens_v.jpg *License:* Public Domain *Contributors:* Acer11, G.dallorto, Gabor~commonswiki, Schaengel89~commonswiki, 竹麦魚 (Searobin) 31

Figure 15 *Source:* https://en.wikipedia.org/w/index.php?title=File:Templar.jpg *License:* Public Domain *Contributors:* AndreasPraefcke, Bibi Saint-Pol, Caveman80, Cirt, Ecelan, EvaK, G.dallorto, Lysis~commonswiki, Mattes, Outsider80, Rd232, Semnoz, Shakko, Un1c0s bot~commonswiki, Warburg 34

Figure 16 *Source:* https://en.wikipedia.org/w/index.php?title=File:Molay.jpg *License:* Public Domain *Contributors:* Bukvoed, Elonka, Massimop, Mu, Nicke L, Siebrand, UDScott, Warburg 35

Figure 17 *Source:* https://en.wikipedia.org/w/index.php?title=File:Templars_Burning.jpg *License:* Public Domain *Contributors:* AndreasPraefcke, Andrew Gray, Bohème, Butko, Darsie, Elonka, G.dallorto, Jheald, Jibi44, Johnbod, Judithcomm, Lotje, Mattes, Mel22, Moeby1, Olivier, Paris 16, Pline, Quibik, Shakko, Siren-Com, Thuresson, Un1c0s bot~commonswiki, 1 anonymous edits 37

Image *Source:* https://en.wikipedia.org/w/index.php?title=File:Emblem_of_the_Papacy_SE.svg *License:* Public Domain *Contributors:* Cronholm144 created this image using a file by User:Hautala - File:Emblem of Vatican City State.svg, who had created his 62

Image *Source:* https://en.wikipedia.org/w/index.php?title=File:Gesupietrochiave.jpg *License:* Public Domain *Contributors:* Alaniaris, AndreasPraefcke, Creert, Eusebius, G.dallorto, JuTa, Leyo, Riccardov, Sailko, Thomas Gun, Walpole, 1 anonymous edits 62

Figure 18 *Source:* https://en.wikipedia.org/w/index.php?title=File:Hugues_de_Payens_(Versailles).jpg *License:* GNU Free Documentation License *Contributors:* Andronicus92, Bohème, BotMultichill, Bukk, Charlik, Ecummenic, Frank C. Müller, Julien Demade, MGA73bot2, Marcok, Vicipaedianus x, Yopie, Максим Підліснюк 66

Figure 19 *Source:* https://en.wikipedia.org/w/index.php?title=File:JacquesdeMolay.jpg *License:* Public Domain *Contributors:* DIREKTOR, Hydrargyrum, Mu, World Imaging, 1 anonymous edits 66

Image *Source:* https://en.wikipedia.org/w/index.php?title=File:Armoiries_Ugo_dei_Pagani.svg *Contributors:* - 63

Image *Source:* https://en.wikipedia.org/w/index.php?title=File:Armoiries_Robert_de_Craon.svg *License:* Creative Commons Attribution-Sharealike 3.0,2.5,2.0,1.0 *Contributors:* user:Odejea, user:Odejea 63

Image *Source:* https://en.wikipedia.org/w/index.php?title=File:Armoiries_Evrard_des_Barres.svg *License:* Creative Commons Attribution-Sharealike 3.0,2.5,2.0,1.0 *Contributors:* user:Odejea, user:Odejea 63

Image *Source:* https://en.wikipedia.org/w/index.php?title=File:Armoiries_Bernard_de_Tramelay.svg *License:* Creative Commons Attribution-Sharealike 3.0,2.5,2.0,1.0 *Contributors:* user:Odejea, user:Odejea 63

Image *Source:* https://en.wikipedia.org/w/index.php?title=File:Armoiries_Bertrand_de_Blanquefort.svg *License:* Creative Commons Attribution-Sharealike 3.0,2.5,2.0,1.0 *Contributors:* user:Odejea, user:Odejea 64

Image *Source:* https://en.wikipedia.org/w/index.php?title=File:Armoiries_Philippe_de_Milly.svg *License:* Creative Commons Attribution-Sharealike 3.0,2.5,2.0,1.0 *Contributors:* user:Odejea, user:Odejea 64

Image *Source:* https://en.wikipedia.org/w/index.php?title=File:Armoiries_Eudes_de_Saint-Amand.svg *License:* Creative Commons Attribution-Sharealike 3.0,2.5,2.0,1.0 *Contributors:* user:Odejea, user:Odejea 64

Image *Source:* https://en.wikipedia.org/w/index.php?title=File:Armoiries_Arnaud_de_Toroge.svg *License:* Creative Commons Attribution-Sharealike 3.0,2.5,2.0,1.0 *Contributors:* user:Odejea, user:Odejea 64

Image *Source:* https://en.wikipedia.org/w/index.php?title=File:Armoiries_Philippe_du_Plaissis.svg *License:* Creative Commons Attribution-Sharealike 3.0,2.5,2.0,1.0 *Contributors:* user:Odejea, user:Odejea 64

Image *Source:* https://en.wikipedia.org/w/index.php?title=File:Armoiries_Guillaume_de_Chartres.svg *License:* Creative Commons Attribution-Sharealike 3.0,2.5,2.0,1.0 *Contributors:* user:Odejea, user:Odejea 64
Image *Source:* https://en.wikipedia.org/w/index.php?title=File:Armoiries_Pierre_de_Montaigu.svg *License:* Creative Commons Attribution-Sharealike 3.0,2.5,2.0,1.0 *Contributors:* user:Odejea, user:Odejea 64
Image *Source:* https://en.wikipedia.org/w/index.php?title=File:Blason_Bures-sur-Yvette.svg *License:* Public Domain *Contributors:* BotMultichill, De728631, Flying jacket, Liné1, Massimop, VIGNERON, Wikimandia 64
Image *Source:* https://en.wikipedia.org/w/index.php?title=File:Armoiries_Guillaume_de_Saunhac.svg *License:* Creative Commons Attribution-Sharealike 3.0,2.5,2.0,1.0 *Contributors:* user:Odejea, user:Odejea 64
Image *Source:* https://en.wikipedia.org/w/index.php?title=File:Armoiries_Renaud_de_Vichiers.svg *License:* Creative Commons Attribution-Sharealike 3.0,2.5,2.0,1.0 *Contributors:* user:Odejea, user:Odejea 64
Image *Source:* https://en.wikipedia.org/w/index.php?title=File:Armoiries_Guillaume_de_Beaujeu.svg *License:* Creative Commons Attribution-Sharealike 3.0,2.5,2.0,1.0 *Contributors:* user:Odejea, user:Odejea 64
Image *Source:* https://en.wikipedia.org/w/index.php?title=File:Armoiries_Thibaud_Gaudin.svg *License:* Creative Commons Attribution-Sharealike 3.0,2.5,2.0,1.0 *Contributors:* user:Odejea, user:Odejea 64
Image *Source:* https://en.wikipedia.org/w/index.php?title=File:Coat_of_arms_Jacques_de_Molay.svg *License:* Creative Commons Attribution-Sharealike 3.0,2.5,2.0,1.0 *Contributors:* Odejea, AnonMoos 65
Figure 20 *Source:* https://en.wikipedia.org/w/index.php?title=File:Forteresses_templières.png *License:* Creative Commons Attribution-ShareAlike 3.0 Unported *Contributors:* AnonMoos, Ayack, BotMultichill, Cplakidas, Electionworld, Kurpfalzbilder.de, Odejea, Scorpius59, Skim, 1 anonymous edits 69
Figure 21 *Source:* https://en.wikipedia.org/w/index.php?title=File:Templerorden_in_Europa_1300.png *Contributors:* Marco Zanoli (sidonius (talk) 20:42, 5 January 2009 (UTC)) 69
Figure 22 *Source:* https://en.wikipedia.org/w/index.php?title=File:International_Organisation_of_Good_Templars_membership_certificate_1868.jpg *License:* Public Domain *Contributors:* Hatch & Co., New York (lithography). Lyman T. Moore, Lawton, Michigan (publisher). 74
Figure 23 *Source:* https://en.wikipedia.org/w/index.php?title=File:Losjehuset_Maihaugen.jpg *License:* Public Domain *Contributors:* Mahlum 75
Figure 24 *Source:* https://en.wikipedia.org/w/index.php?title=File:IOGT_Membership_Card.jpg *License:* GNU Free Documentation License *Contributors:* Bmbaker88 76
Figure 25 *Source:* https://en.wikipedia.org/w/index.php?title=File:Thomas_Dunckerley.jpg *Contributors:* Christophe Dioux, Claíomh Solais, Fiddlersmouth 81
Figure 26 *Source:* https://en.wikipedia.org/w/index.php?title=File:Structure_of_Masonic_appendant_bodies_in_England_and_Wales.jpg *License:* Creative Commons Attribution-Sharealike 3.0 *Contributors:* User:Cyan22 82
Figure 27 *Source:* https://en.wikipedia.org/w/index.php?title=File:KT-cross-UK.gif *License:* Creative Commons Attribution-Sharealike 3.0 *Contributors:* Timothy Titus 83
Figure 28 *Source:* https://en.wikipedia.org/w/index.php?title=File:Knight-Saint-Paul.jpg *License:* Creative Commons Attribution-Sharealike 3.0 *Contributors:* Timothy Titus 84
Figure 29 *Source:* https://en.wikipedia.org/w/index.php?title=File:Cross_of_the_Knights_Hospitaller.png *License:* Public Domain *Contributors:* Own work 85
Figure 30 *Source:* https://en.wikipedia.org/w/index.php?title=File:Crosscrown.svg *License:* Public Domain *Contributors:* Frater5 86
Figure 31 *Source:* https://en.wikipedia.org/w/index.php?title=File:Templar_induction_2009_3.jpg *License:* Creative Commons Attribution 2.0 *Contributors:* Templar_induction_2009.jpg: Danny Thompson from Winter Park, USA derivative work: GrapedApe (talk) 87

License

Creative Commons Attribution-Share Alike 3.0
//creativecommons.org/licenses/by-sa/3.0/

Index

Abbey of St. Michael, 72
Abbot, 5
Absolution, 43
Absolve, 37
Acre, Israel, 7, 68
ACTIVE, 76
ADIC India, 77
ADIC Sri Lanka, 77
Ad providam, 2, 10, 45, 61, 67
Afonso I of Portugal, 59
Al-Aqsa Mosque, 4
Alberic of Trois-Fontaines, 15
All Ceylon Young Mens Muslim Association Conference, 77
Allied Masonic Degrees, 87
Amalric of Tyre, 29
Amardeep (organisation), 77
ANDO, 77
André de Montbard, 4, 5, 47, 56, 64
Andrew Michael Ramsay, 79, 80
Anglosphere, 80
Anjou, 11
Antient Grand Lodge of England, 80, 81
Anti-Masonry, 88
Antioch, 11
Apostasy, 34
Apostolic notary, 42
Apostolic prefect, 62
Apostolic Syndic, 62
Apostolic vicariate, 62
Apostolic visitor, 62
Aquitania, 40
Archbishop, 62
Architecture, 16
Argentina, 74
Ark of the Covenant, 18, 84
Armand de Périgord, 47, 64
Arnold of Torroja, 48, 64
Arville, Loir-et-Cher, 70
Arwad, 7, 29, 68
Arwad Island, 7
Ashkelon, 24
ASPAT, 77
Assassins Creed, 18

Assistant at the Pontifical Throne, 62
Atbash, 34
Atlit, 7
Atmosphere F, 77
Augustinian, 36
Auxiliary bishop, 62
Avignon, 8
Ayyubid dynasty, 7

Baldock, 71
Baldwin II of Jerusalem, 4
Baldwin IV of Jerusalem, 24
Ban Borić, 55
Banditry, 4
Banking, 3, 6, 26
Bannockburn, 18
Baphomet, 3, 9, 18, 33, 34, 46, 61, 68
Barbara Frale, 11, 37, 39, 43
Barbens, 70
Barrister, 16
Bar-sur-Seine, 68
Battle of Arsuf, 2
Battle of Bannockburn, 89
Battle of Hattin, 2, 7, 14, 27
Battle of La Forbie, 95
Battle of Legnica, 2
Battle of Marj Ayyun, 2
Battle of Montgisard, 2, 6, 24, 27
Belen Pass, 28
Bérenger Fredoli, 39
Berlin, 72
Bermuda, 74
Bernard de Tremelay, 14, 63
Bernard of Clairvaux, 1, 5
Bertrand de Blanchefort, 64
Birmingham, 74
Bishop Emeritus, 62
Bishop in the Catholic Church, 62
Blacksmith, 13
Blanzac-Porcheresse, 70
Blasphemy, 41
Bosnia-Herzegovina, 76
Brain Society, 77
Brckovljani, 72

Bristol, 71
British Guyana, 74
British Honduras, 74
British people, 7
Broken Sword, 18
Bulgaria, 76
Burma, 75
Burriana, 49
Burundi, 76

Cambrai, 42
Cambridgeshire, 71
Cameley, 71
Cardinal (Catholic Church), 62
Cardinal (Catholicism), 39
Cardinal Vicar, 62
Castello della Magione, 72
Castellote, 70
Castelo Branco, Portugal, 59
Castelo de Monsanto, 70
Castle of Alcañices, 70
Castle of Almourol, 70
Castle of Montalbán, 70
Castle of San Servando, 70
Castle of Villalba, 70
Category:Catholic chivalric orders, 3, 46, 61, 68
Category:Catholic Church offices, 62
Category:Knights Templar, 2, 45, 61, 67
Catholic, 3
Catholic Church, 1, 62
Catholic Encyclopedia, 19
Celles, Cantal, 70
Champagne, France, 29
Chaplain, 13, 34
Chaplain of His Holiness, 62
Charles Greenstreet Addison, 20, 93
Charles II of Naples, 28
Chastel Blanc, 68
Château de Chinon, 29
Château Pèlerin, 68
Cheque, 6
Chess, 26
Chinon, 39, 40
Chinon Parchment, 11, 37, **39**
Chivalry, 80
Christ, 2, 45, 61, 67
Christendom, 3, 5
Christian cross, 3, 34
Christian finance, 3
Christianity, 80
Christians, 4
Christopher L. Hodapp, 21, 90
Church hierarchy, 62
Church of Santa Maria do Olival, 70
Church of St. Mary the Virgin, Baldock, 71

Church of the Holy Sepulchre, 17
Chwarszczany, 72
Circa, 1, 6, 16
Cistercian, 36
Cistercian Order, 5
Cistercians, 11
CITEREFBarber1993, 91, 92
CITEREFBarber1994, 91, 92
CITEREFBarber2006, 91
CITEREFBurman1990, 91, 92
CITEREFMartin2005, 91, 92
CITEREFMoeller1912, 91
CITEREFNicholson2001, 91, 92
CITEREFRead2001, 91, 92
CITEREFSobecki2006, 91
Clontarf Castle, 72
Coadjutor bishop, 62
Coercion, 9
Commandery (feudalism), 87
Commandry, 3, 68
Commons:Category:International Organisation of Good Templars, 78
Commons:Category:Knights Templar, 21, 71
Commons:Category:Knights Templar (Freemasonry), 90
Conspiracy theory, 32
Convent of the Order of Christ, 9, 70
Cornwall, 71
Coulommiers, Seine-et-Marne, 68
Council of Nablus, 4
Council of Troyes, 5, 14
Council of Vienne, 10, 31
County Dublin, 72
County of Portugal, 59
County of Roussillon, 48
County of Tripoli, 11
County Wexford, 72
Cressing Temple, 71
Croatia, 11, 55, 76
Cross, 1
Cross and Crown, 86
Cross pattée, 83
Crown of Aragon, 11, 48
Crown of Castile, 59
Crusader states, 13
Crusades, 2, 3, 46
Cryptic Masonry, 88
Cult image, 41
Cumbria, 71
Cyprus, 6, 27–29
Czech lands, 49
Czech Republic, 49, 72, 76

Daniel Cady, 73
David Bryce, 89
Death by burning, 10

Degrees, 82
Dei gesta per Francos, 92
De:Karl Gotthelf von Hund und Altengrotkau, 95
Denny Abbey, 71
DeWitt Clinton, 80
Digital object identifier, 19
Diocesan bishop, 62
Diocese of Soissons, 42
Diocese of Tours, 40
DMOZ, 21
DNT (temperance organization), 77

Eastern Europe, 14
Eastern Mediterranean, 26
East India, 74
Edinburgh, 89
EGTYF Macedonia, 77
Encryption, 34
Encyclopædia Britannica Eleventh Edition, 21
England, 31, 80
England and Wales, 79
Esotericism, 18
Essene, 34
Essex, 71
Estonia, 76
Estonian Temperance Union, 76

Étienne Baluze, 11, 39, 43, 94

Eucharist, 33
Euphemia, 34
Europe, 68, 74
Everard des Barres, 51, 63
Execution by burning, 36

Faciens misericordiam, 2, 39, 45, 61, 67
Famagusta, 68
Faroe Islands, 76
Finland, 76
First Crusade, 4, 86
First Crusader Kingdom of Jerusalem, 68
Fortification, 3
Fortress of Klis, 72
FORUT Germany, 76
FORUT Norway, 77
Foucaults Pendulum, 18
Foulques de Villaret, 8
France, 39
France in the Middle Ages, 40
Franck Gordon, 21, 90
Franco-Mongol alliance, 7
Fraternal and service organizations, 73
Fraternal organization, 73
Frederick II, Holy Roman Emperor, 7
Freemasonry, 18, 73, 79, 89

Freemasons, 89
Free Youth Bulgaria, 76
Friday the 13th, 8
FSNU-MHF, 76
Fulk V, Count of Anjou, 47

Gallica, 20
Gambia, 76
Garway Church, 71
Gary Lachman, 93
Gaza City, 24
Geoffrey de Charney, 36, 51
Geoffrey of Paris, 91
Geoffroi de Charney, 10
Geoffroy de Charney, 40
Gerard de Ridefort, 27, 56, 64
Gérard de Ridefort, 14
Germain-François Poullain de Saint-Foix, 91, 93, 94
Germany, 30, 72
GGPF Italy, 77
Ghana, 76
Gilbert de Lacy, 50
Gilbert Erail, 53, 64
Gilbert Horal, 48, 57
Glogovnica, 72
Gnostic, 34
God, 10, 80
Godfrey de Saint-Omer, 4, 47
Gonfanon, 16
Gora, Croatia, 72
Gornji Slatinik, 72
Grand Encampment of Knights Templar of the United States, 79
Grand Lodge of Scotland, 89
Grand Master (Masonic), 89
Grand master (order), 39, 63
Grand Masters of the Knights Templar, 2, 11, 45–48, 57, 61, **61**, 67
Grenada, 74
Gualdim Pais, 59
Guillaume de Beaujeu, 47, 64
Guillaume de Chartres, 64
Guillaume de Sonnac, 64
Guinea-Bissau, 76

Hans Prutz, 38
Heavy cavalry, 13
Henry II, King of England, 94
Henry the Navigator, 31
Herefordshire, 71
Heresy, 11, 29, 33
Hertfordshire, 71
Hierarchy of the Catholic Church, 62
Highwaymen, 4
Hiram Abiff, 88

Historical document, 39
History of the Knights Templar, 2, **23**, 45, 61, 67
History (U.S. TV channel), 19, 38, 89, 90, 93
Holy Grail, 18
Holy Land, 3–5, 27, 68
Holy Mass, 34
Holy Roman Empire, 12
Holy Royal Arch, 79, 81, 82, 90
Holy See, 3, 11, 36
Horses in warfare, 5
Hospitallers, 36
Hrvatska Dubica, 72
Hugh, Count of Champagne, 47
Hugh de Paduinan, 50
Hugh J. Schonfield, 34
Hugues de Pairaud, 40, 51, 54
Hugues de Payens, 2, 4, 14, 34, 47, 63, 66
Humbert de Pairaud, 50, 51, 54, 56
Hungary, 55
Hyères, 68

Iberian Peninsula, 30, 31
Iceland, 74, 77
Icelandic Temperance Youth, 77
Idanha-a-Nova, 70
Idolatry, 8, 9, 34
Indiana Jones and the Last Crusade, 18
In Hoc Signo Vinces, 86
Initiation ceremony, 3
Inner Temple, 16, 17, 71
Inns of Court, 16, 17
Inquisition, 9
International Academy of Sobriety, 77
International Order of Good Templars, 18
International Organisation of Good Templars, **73**
International Standard Book Number, 19–21, 38, 90
IOGT Belgium, 76
IOGT Burundi, 76
IOGT Czech Republic, 76
IOGT Denmark, 76
IOGT England and Wales, 77
IOGT Estonia, 76
IOGT Faroe Islands, 76
IOGT Finland, 76
IOGT – Healthy Lifestyle Society, 77
IOGT Gambia, 76
IOGT Germany, 76
IOGT Ghana, 76
IOGT Guinea-Bissau, 76
IOGT Iceland, 77
IOGT Junior in Island, 77
IOGT Junior Organisation, 77
IOGT Kenya, 77

IOGT Latvia, 77
IOGT Norway, 77
IOGT-NTO, 77
IOGT Scotland, 77
IOGT Senegal, 77
IOGT Sierra Leone, 77
IOGT Switzerland, 77
IOGT Thailand, 77
IOGT-USA, 77
IOGT Vietnam, 77
IOTT South, 77
Israel, 7
Italy, 11, 30
Ivanhoe, 18

Jacques de Molay, 2, 8, 14, 28, 35, 36, 39, 65, 66, 88, 91
Jaffa, 4
JAF Latvia, 77
Jamaica, 74
James St Clair-Erskine, 3rd Earl of Rosslyn, 89
Jerusalem, 1, 4, 12, 46, 74
John the Baptist, 9, 34
Joseph Malins, 74
Journal of Medieval History, 19, 43
JUNIS, 77
Jurand, 58
Juvente Estonia, 76
Juvente Germany, 76
Juvente Norway, 77
Juvente Switzerland, 77

Karl Gotthelf von Hund, 80
Keele, 71
Kent, 71
Kenya, 77
Khwarazmian dynasty, 7
Killed in action, 63, 64
KiM Switzerland, 77
Kingdom of Aragon, 31, 36, 48
Kingdom of Jerusalem, 1
Kingdom of Leon, 59
Kingdom of Majorca, 48
Kingdom of Navarre, 48
Kingdom of Portugal, 31
Kingdom of Valencia, 48
King Henry II of Cyprus, 29
Kiss, 41
Klub Lijecenih Alkoholikar Opcine, 76
Klub Mladih Juvente, 76
Knight, 4
Knight Kadosh, 88
Knights Hospitaller, 7, 8, 15, 18, 27–29, 31, 79, 80
Knights of Jericho, 73
Knights of Malta, 79

Knights Templar, **1**, 2, 26, 39, 45, 46, 61, 63, 67, 68, 79, 89
Knights Templar (Freemasonry), **79**
Knights Templar in England, 2, 11, 45, 61, 67
Knights Templar in France, 2, 45, 61, 67
Knights Templar in popular culture, 3, 46, 61, 68
Knights Templar in Portugal, 2, 45, 61, 67
Knights Templar in Scotland, 2, 45, 61, 67
Knights Templar in Spain, 2, 45, 61, 67
Knights Templars, 19
Knights Templar Seal, 1, 2, 45, 61, 67
Knights Templar Trial, 15
Kolossi Castle, 68

La Couvertoirade, 70
Languedoc, 29
Lanka Jatilka Sarvodaya Shramadana Movement, 77
La Rochelle, 32, 68
Latin language, 3
Latin Rule, 2, 14, 45, 61, 67
Latvia, 77
Lawyer, 16
Legend, 18
Lérida, 70
Letter of credit, 6
Leverett Coon, 74
Light cavalry, 13
Limassol, 7
Lincolnshire, 71
LINK (temperance organization), 76
List of history journals, 37
List of Knights Templar, 2, 45, **45**, 61, 67
List of Knights Templar sites, 2, 45, 61, 67, **67**
List of Portuguese monarchs, 59
List of rulers of Bohemia, 49
List of Temperance organizations, 17
Lithuania, 77
Lithuanian Temperance Society, 77
Lithuanian Temperance Youth Federation, 77
Little Maplestead, 71
Lodge Mother Kilwinning, 80
London, 71, 79
Louis VII of France, 14, 25
Lovčić, 72
Lynn Picknett, 20

Madras, 74
Madras Social Service Guild, 77
Major archbishop, 62
Malacca, 74
Malcolm Barber, 19, 20, 33, 38, 91
Malta, 74
Maltese Cross, 25, 85
Mamluk Sultanate (Cairo), 7

Mantle (vesture), 3
Mark Masons Hall, London, 79, 83
Martyr, 15
Masonic bodies, 18, 80
Masonic body, 79
Masonic lodge, 73, 80
Matthew Paris, 16
Medieval Inquisition, 15, 33, 39
Metropolitan bishop, 62
Metz, 12, 68
Middle East, 35
Middle Temple, 16, 17, 71
Midlothian, 72
Military campaign, 14
Military fiat, 31
Military order (monastic society), 1, 3, 18, 46, 61, 68
Military order (society), 3, 7
Milites Templi, 2, 45, 61, 67
Militia Dei, 2, 45, 61, 67
Miravet, 70
Moderator of the curia, 62
Modern Eastern Catholic churches, 62
Monasticism, 4, 11
Monastic state, 8
Monastic vows, 25
Money, 26, 31
Montescaglioso, 72
Montpellier, 42
Multinational corporation, 3, 6
Murcia, 48
Muslim, 6

NADA India Foundation, 77
Našice, 72
National Geographic Channel, 93
National Treasure (film), 18, 32
National Youth Council of IOGT England, 77
Near East, 8
Netherlands, 75, 77
Nicolas Cage, 32
Nigeria, 75
Noble knights, 13
NOM (temperance organization), 77
Non nobis, 3, 46, 61, 68
Non-Violent Direct Action Group, 77
Normandy, 10, 40
North Yorkshire, 71
Norway, 77
Notre Dame de Paris, 10
Nova Rača, 72
Nova Ves, 72
Nuncio, 62
Nykterhetsrörelsens Scoutförbund, 77

Oak Island, 32

107

Occitania, 48
Odo de St Amand, 64
Omne Datum Optimum, 2, 3, 5, 45, 61, 67
Order of Christ (Portugal), 3, 9, 11, 31, 36, 46, 59, 61, 68
Order of DeMolay, 88
Order of Holy Royal Arch Knight Templar Priests, 90
Order of Knight Masons, 87
Order of Knights Beneficent of the Holy City, 90
Order of Malta (Freemasonry), 18
Order of Mark Master Masons, 79
Order of Montesa, 3, 31, 36, 46, 61, 68
Order of precedence in the Catholic Church, 62
Order of St. Thomas of Acon, 90
Order of the Solar Temple, 89
Order of the Temple - Great Priory of Ireland, 79
Order of the Temple - Great Priory of Scotland, 79
Ordination, 13
Ordo Templi Orientis, 89
Oriskany Falls, 73
Ottoman Empire, 7
Otton de Grandson, 28
Outremer, 4, 26, 27, 40
Oxfordshire, 71

Paganism, 34
Paleographer, 39
Palestine (region), 25
Panama, 75
Papal bull, 2, 3, 5, 35, 45, 61, 67
Papal legate, 62
Papal majordomo, 62
Papal States, 1
Parable of the Good Samaritan, 95
Parchment, 39
Paris, 30
Parzival, 18
Pastoralis Praeeminentiae, 2, 9, 30, 45, 61, 67
Patrick Levaye, 21
PCDP-Cambodia, 77
Pedro de Montaigu, 64
Peniscola Castle, 70
Perugia, 72
Philip IV of France, 3, 8, 11, 37, 39, 42, 43
Philip of Nablus, 64
Phillipe de Plessis, 64
Pierre de Montaigu, 48
Pierre Dupuy (scholar), 11, 43, 94
Piers Paul Read, 20
Pilgrimage, 4
Pinterest, 95
Poggibonsi, 72

Poitou, 11, 40
Poland, 72, 77
Pombal, Portugal, 70
Ponferrada, 70
Pontius de Cruce, 55
Pope, 62
Pope Benedict XVI, 43
Pope Boniface VIII, 28
Pope Clement V, 3, 8, 35, 39
Pope Eugene III, 14
Pope Innocent II, 5
Portal:Catholicism, 3, 46, 61, 63, 68
Portugal, 9, 25, 36, 74, 77
Power behind the throne, 27
Power of attorney, 25
Prats-de-Mollo, 60
Preceptory, 82
Premier Grand Lodge of England, 80
Primate (bishop), 62
Prince Charles Edward Stuart, 80
Prince Edward Augustus, Duke of Kent and Strathearn, 81
Principality of Catalonia, 48
Priory, 83
Prisoner of war, 64
Prussia, 29

Qumran, 34

Raittiuden Ystävät ry., 76
Reconquista, 2, 25
Red Cross of Constantine, 18, 87
Relapse, 35
Relic, 18, 34
Religious habit, 14
Religious order, 23
Religious vows, 16
Renaissance Magazine, 19
Renaud de Vichier, 51
Renaud de Vichiers, 64
Rhodes, Greece, 8
Richard de Bures, 64
Richard I of England, 25
Richerenches, 70
Rituals, 81
Robert de Craon, 51, 63
Robert de Miliaco, 51
Robert IV de Sablé, 52, 64
Robert of St. Albans, 50
Robert the Bruce, 18, 89
Roche-Guillaume, 28
Roger of Howden, 50
Roman Catholic Archdiocese of Sens, 9
Roman Catholic Church, 11
Roslin, Midlothian, 89
Rosslyn Chapel, 89

Rothley, Leicestershire, 71
Rothley Temple, 71
Royal Arch Masonry, 88
Royal Order of Scotland, 89
Russia, 77

Sacrament, 34
Sacred Military Constantinian Order of Saint George, 18
Saint Blaise, 68
Sainte-Eulalie-de-Cernon, 70
Saint-Gaugery, 42
Saint Peter, 62
Saint Ursula, 34
Saladin, 6, 24
Saladin tithe, 50
Saltire, 84
San Bevignate, 72
San Pietro alla Magione, Siena, 72
SantAngelo in Pescheria, 39
Satanism, 30
Scandal (theology), 11
Scotland, 18
Scottish Knights Templar, 89
Scottish Rite, 80, 88, 89
Sean Martin (writer and director), 19, 38
Second Crusade, 14
Second Temple of Jerusalem, 84
Segovia, 70
Seine, 36
Senegal, 77
Senj, 72
Sergeac, 70
Sermoneta, 72
Sharan Newman, 19
Shipley, West Sussex, 71
Shock troops, 5
Siege of Acre (1189), 14
Siege of Acre (1189–1191), 2
Siege of Acre (1291), 2, 28
Siege of Al-Dāmūs, 2
Siege of Ascalon, 2, 14
Siege of Jerusalem (1187), 7
Siege of Ruad, 7
Siena, 72
Sierra Leone, 74, 77
Sinclair (surname), 89
Sinuli Finland, 76
Sixth Crusade, 7
Skerries, Dublin, 72
Slavonia, 55
Slovakia, 77
SOBER Tanzania, 77
SOBER Uganda, 77
Sociedade Anti-Alcoólica Portuguesa, 77
Sodomy, 33, 41

Solomons Temple, 4, 5
Somerset, 71
Sophia (wisdom), 34
Soure Castle, 70
South Africa, 74, 77
Sovereign Great Priory of the Knights Templar of Canada, 79
Sovereign Military Order of Malta, 3, 46, 61, 68
Sovereign Military Order of the Temple of Jerusalem, 89
Spain, 25
Squire, 13
Sri Lanka, 74, 77
Sri Lanka Interactive Media Group, 77
Sri Lanka Temperance Association, 77
Staffordshire, 71
Standing army, 8
State of the Teutonic Order, 8
St. Clair (disambiguation), 89
St. Cyriac in Thermis, 39
St. Helena, 74
St Jamess, 79
St Jamess Street, 79
St Michaels Mount, 71
Stratford, London, 71
Success Lodge No.1 I.O.G.T., 77
Suffragan bishop, 62
Supreme Order of Christ, 3, 11, 46, 61, 68
Surcoat, 14
Syracuse, New York, 74
Syria, 7

Tactics of heavy cavalry using lances, 5
Tanzania, 77
Tartous, 68
Tartus, 7, 29
Tempelhof, 72
Temperance Association of Orissa, 77
Temperance movement, 18, 73
Temperance Youth Club of Sri Lanka, 77
Temperance Youth Organisation of Sri Lanka, 77
Templars, 21
Templars Square, 71
Template:Catholic Church hierarchy sidebar, 63
Template:Knights Templar, 3, 46, 62, 68
Template talk:Catholic Church hierarchy sidebar, 63
Template talk:Knights Templar, 3, 46, 62, 68
Temple Balsall, 71
Temple Bar, London, 16
Temple Bruer, 71
Temple Church, 17, 71
Temple Church, Bristol, 71

Temple Cloud, 71
Templecombe, 71
Temple Cowley, 71
Temple Dinsley, 71
Temple Ewell, 71
Temple, London, 16
Temple, Midlothian, 72
Temple Mills, 71
Temple Mount, 1, 4, 5, 18
Temple Newsam, 71
Temple of Solomon, 2, 45, 61, 67
Temple (Paris), 70
Temple Sowerby, 71
Temple tube station, 16, 71
Templstejn, 72
Ten Duinen Abbey, 15
Territorial abbey, 63
Territorial prelate, 62
Teutonic Knights, 27, 29
Teutonic Order, 7, 8
Thailand, 77
The Bahamas, 74
The Da Vinci Code, 18
The Degree of Knight of the Temple (Order of the Temple), 18
The Holy Blood and the Holy Grail, 32
The Last Templar (miniseries), 18
The NAN Foundation, 77
The Templar House, Toledo, 70
The Temple (London), 71
Thibaud Gaudin, 57, 64
Thomas Bérard, 49, 64
Thomas Dunckerley, 79–81
Tiberias, 27
Titular bishop, 62
Together against Drugs, 77
Tomar, 59, 70
Tortosa, 7
Torture, 33, 41
Total abstinence, 73
Toul, 68
Tours, 30
Trials of the Knights Templar, 2, 9, 40, 45, 61, 67
Trinidad, 74
Trinity, 82
Troia (FG), 42
Turks & Caicos Islands, 77

Uganda, 77
Ukraine, 77
Ukrainian Society for Temperance & Health, 77
UNESCO, 9
Ungdomens Nykterhetsförbund, 77
United Grand Lodge of England, 79

United States, 80, 88
Usury, 26
Utica, New York, 73

Valvisciolo Abbey, 72
Vatican Secret Archives, 11, 37, 39, 43
Vietnam, 77
Vineyard, 8
Virje, 72
Vižinada, 72
Vox in excelso, 2, 10, 45, 61, 67
Vrana, Zadar County, 72

Wales, 74
Warmund, Patriarch of Jerusalem, 4
Warwickshire, 71
War with the English, 8
Wesley Bailey, 73
Westerdale, 71
Western Europe, 14
West Sussex, 71
West Yorkshire, 71
Wikipedia:Citation needed, 26, 27, 29, 35, 36, 54, 57, 60
William de Ferrers, 3rd Earl of Derby, 50
William Marshal, 1st Earl of Pembroke, 50
Wiltshire, 71
Wisdom, 34
Witchcraft, 18
Wolfram von Eschenbach, 18
World Heritage Site, 9
World War I, 7
Worship, 33

Xivert, 70

York Rite, 18, 80, 87
Youth Antidrug Federation, 77
Youth organizations, 88
Youth Temperance Movement Better, 77

Zamora (Spain), 70
Zdelja, 72
Zerubbabel, 84

www.ingramcontent.com/pod-product-compliance
Lightning Source LLC
Chambersburg PA
CBHW031947070426
42453CB00007BA/442